Incredible
But True

by

Jack L. Rawlins

Dedication

This book is dedicated to my wife Elizabeth, who lived through the stories along with me over fifty–two years of happiness, excitement, and (sometimes) terror.

ISBN 0-9664129-0-7

Table of Contents

Prologue

Some pretty weird things can happen to a fellow as he meanders through life–or to others who happen to be in his immediate neighborhood—and I feel that a few of those which happened to or around me are worthy of mention for one reason or another. Hence, this collection of stories.

You will find absolutely no continuity from one story to another, so putting the book aside should prove simple (in case you need to attend church or any of your other wants whilst reading).

All of the characters in the stories are *not* fictional, and efforts have been earnestly made to have them resemble themselves, living or dead. Without exaggeration or brushing over any little faults that may have been present in their characters, it has been our effort to maintain an objective view of the proceedings in every case, as well as of the personality involved. No mean task, I might add.

In any event, I hope you will find the various episodes as humorous, interesting and/or terrifying as all of the participants did at the time.   —*J.L.R.*

GEORGE

The river flowed serenely past the cut–banks and sand islands, headed east toward the horizon and Mozambique. North, one–half mile and more across the lazy waters, the Zambia shore was plainly visible through the light dawn haze, the escarpments rising blue–green behind it into the African sky. It was nearing the end of the dry season now, and the river was low. Still, more than 1,200,000 gallons of the turbid waters were passing each minute. The side channels were becoming dry, the hippos leaving them to pod up out in the river's main currents. The bush along the banks on the riverine flood plain was stark, brittle–grey and leafless, awaiting the rains that would come in a month or two. Only the majestic *acacia albidas* had leaves. Leaves and seed pods. Scimitar–curved yellow pods filled with seeds full of protein. The pods were ripe, and had begun falling.

A massive grey bulk moved easily through the thorn bush that framed the clearing, ponderously picked its way gracefully though a jumble of wind–fallen logs and out into the open beneath the acacias. As the elephant moved, his long trunk was busy, plucking pods from among the dry leaves and stuffing them casually into the maw between the sweep of his white tusks in a rhythmic, ceaseless motion. George was hungry.

The dry yellow grass no longer held nutrition, the foliage was gone from the brush and smaller trees. For millennia the protein in the pods had carried George and his kind through the dry seasons. This plain, with the canopy of pod–laden acacias shading it from the fierce African sun, was a dry season haven. For all of his forty years it had "belonged" to George and his friends during the winter months when they came down from the escarpments and canyons to feed on the flood plains of the great river.

Others had come to the banks of the Zambezi this spring. Come with their land rovers and toyotas, tents and tables. George's eyes blinked slowly as he fed, a trickle of tear fluid staining each side of his face with a dark dampness. Anything further off than thirty or forty feet, unless it was moving, was beyond his vision. The huge ears, slowly flapping to cool, like giant air conditioners, the blood which flowed through the swollen veins on the back side, were much more acute, as was his trunk. Though he was still several hundred yards away, George heard the camp sounds plainly, as its occupants rose to the new day. He could smell its smells, too, for the wind was right. Humans again. He

2•

was not concerned. He considered them to be, like the leopards and lions that shared the areas, no threat. He calmly continued on his meandering way toward the camp, feeding steadily.

The camp was an elaborate affair: safari tents for officers of the Zimbabwe Parks Department and their families, smaller pup tents for Game Scouts, cooks, and two Air Force pilots encircled a large cooking and dining area, with long tables and several dozen chairs. Not far from the tents a helicopter sat in a small clearing, surrounded by drums of fuel. The pilots had placed their small tent nearby in order to watch over the chopper.

Tent ropes tied to stakes spread from all the tents like the multiple legs of giant green insects. Some tent ropes were tied to convenient tree trunks instead of stakes. Acacia tree trunks. Clotheslines were stretched near the cooking area, and several thatch–enclosed longdrops had been constructed at strategic points. As George came close enough to really see the extent of the camp, he looked about curiously for a long moment, raised his trunk to sniff the many strange odors, then dropped it, resumed feeding, and walked on into camp.

Not everyone was up yet. The two pilots were among those still peacefully asleep as George arrived at their small tent. He hesitated, eyeing the tent, which was small and low to the ground. Casually, he picked up the tent to see what was under it, but he hastily put it back over the one pilot who had been too paralyzed to run. Then, fascinated, he watched the other pilot demonstrate total upward mobility, level off and make long, rapid tracks in the general direction of the South Pole, disappearing over the horizon as apologies came rumbling from George's stomach. Strangled guffaws, one cynic suggested later, but this idea was generally discounted as sour grapes by others in camp. The pilots decided to move their gear to the center of camp—the chopper could jolly well look after itself, they pointed out.

George appeared to be interested, but unruffled. He proceeded to feed his way completely through the camp, pausing twice to poke his head and trunk into the doorways of tents. His own calm demeanor was not reciprocated, nor were his efforts to form any lasting relationships with the occupants of those tents. He had hardly said hello before they had departed through the aperture closest to them and furthest away from him. By the time he reached the far edge of the camp, his wake had begun to resemble a Chinese New Year's parade, *sans* firecrackers. A small entourage of humankind was following—at distances variously regarded as safe—banging on pans, shouting, and making a general uproar. This had the same effect on George as it did on the surrounding bush—none. He kept going, at the same speed, to all appearances oblivious of the din. That was our introduction to George.

"Well, that's the last of *him*," Clem declared as the elephant disappeared into the bush. Clem, a Provincial

Warden from a neighboring district, had been called in like the rest of us to assist in the annual large animal census and the rhino research (which were the reasons for the 'copter).

"I doubt it," Ron, the local warden, replied. "He seemed quite unperturbed. I think he has simply gone to alert his friends that the pods are ripe and falling."

Which turned out to be exactly right. Within two hours George was back, accompanied by five other bulls. They came drifting silently out of the bush. One minute there was nothing there, the next instant a six-ton bull elephant was feeding quietly. They paid no attention to the mob of assorted humans they found ensconced in their feeding grounds, seemed not bothered by the intrusion. This is more than could be said for the humans, who continued to make every possible effort to drive the elephants away from camp—without the slightest success.

George and his friends came and went as they pleased, fed where they pleased, when they pleased. It made for considerable confusion—among the people— around camp. The women especially were upset to look up and see a ten-foot-high bulk bearing down on them. Hasty retreats, wild cries of fear, many long moments of hiding in the deserted cement-block wash house's interior. Dark, dirty and smelly; infested with bats; floor covered with bat droppings; and no windows, only one door.

Contributing to the problem was the fact that George and his friends suffered terribly from insomnia. They hardly ever slept—as far as any of us could tell. One time of day—or night—was about the same as any other to them. It seems a bit ridiculous, I admit, to say that anything weighing more than five tons was underfoot, but that is the plain truth of the matter. Not the whole truth, however. George was also overfoot a good deal of the time. There was enough of him to cover both areas. Our problem, most days, was to make sure that *we* didn't get underfoot. They were awfully big feet.

Big, but not clumsy. Quite the contrary. It was not unknown for yours truly to become thoroughly entangled in the various ropes of our tent on night time forays to or from the longdrop, even when in a state of total sobriety. Some of the resultant falls left me bruised and shaken, not to mention coarsely verbose.

But George had no such trouble with these same ropes, though the possibility was never out of my mind for an instant any night when I awoke to the fact that he was standing among them feeding on acacia pods, stepping over and around the ropes flawlessly. After all, my encounters with the ropes posed no threat to the tent—the bruises were all mine. But George, who outweighed me by more than ten thousand pounds? The mere thought of what would happen to the tent, and incidentally to its two occupants, should he react to any such encounter with even a fraction of the anger and frustration I felt during mine, gave me some pause, I can assure you, on those dark nights when I could look through the open window at five bull elephants feeding within twenty feet of my head, two actually rubbing tusks against the tent.

The fears and trepidation were needless. George was not so clumsy as to stumble over anything as simple as a tent rope, even in the dark. He wandered back and forth through that maze of ropes daily and nightly for four weeks without so much as brushing against one—a feat which I would have been proud to claim as my own.

In all truth, it should be pointed out that since we were the trespassers—not he—it was understandable that he might raise some mild objections to our taking over the area in which his people had fed on the sweet acacia pods for so many millennia. In fact, his gentle but firm insistence on remaining in spite of our invasion did him credit.

With quiet dignity, he made his daily and nightly strolls through the length of our encampment, ignoring us as long as we made no attempt to deter his ponderous purpose, agreeably willing to go out of his way, if necessary, in order to bypass rather than walk through such flimsy human–type obstacles as clothes lines and horizontally tied tent guy ropes. There were some thirty people coming and going in the camp, along with children as young as one year. Not a single thing was broken, torn or stepped on by George and he saw to it that his friends, when they accompanied him, were just as careful.

It was interesting that the one thing we humans could not tolerate was to be tolerated. Even worse was to be tolerated and ignored, and when it was being done by someone who weighed five tons, it was pretty damned obvious, so naturally we couldn't ignore being ignored, if you see what I mean. Therefore, we simply had to do something about all this toleration and ignorance. We were assured by the chief ecologist that there was absolutely nothing to worry about, that we would fence off the camp.

It was a curious confrontation: six highly intelligent, well-educated men versus one elephant. Confidently, the wildlife experts decided that the sleeping area tents should be cabled off, after their earlier methods of elephant frightening proved to be much more people frightening. Their efforts had so far resulted only in a mildly irritated George chasing everyone out of camp. After which, he ate all of the oranges out of a burlap sack left before one of the tents, one by one, topping them off by eating the sack. Thus calmed and returned to his normal good spirits, he continued his interrupted tour of the camp acacias and disappeared. By the time the necessary half-mile of quarter-inch cable had been rounded up, George was back.

The chief ecologist assured us that the single strand of cable would deter the elephants, pointing out that they had always carefully walked around the clothesline and all of the tent ropes. So we spent three hours stringing the cable from tree to tree, pulling it tight, as George watched, chewing absentmindedly on a bush. When the barricade was finished, we all sat down at the mess table to refresh ourselves with a beer and admire our work.

George walked slowly up to inspect this new weirdness from the inscrutable mind of man. Then he turned to walk along its periphery as we nodded, complimenting each other on our wisdom and thorough knowledge of wildlife. After all, we were a field research camp of the Zimbabwe Parks Department and among the world's leading wildlife experts. Then George turned around, ambled back along the cable to where it crossed his usual route, lifted the cable with his trunk and casually walked under it. He went on across the tent area, lifted the cable on that side in the same manner and disappeared into the bush. As we drowned our embarrassment in beer, the old boy returned with his pals to show them the cable. They spent an hour and a half walking back and forth under that fool cable, playfully cavorting. They were obviously delighted with it. Maybe it tickled their backs.

As the days passed, it began to seem to some of us that George was beginning to feel more than just tolerance for all of the camp personnel. Especially after the morning when two adult male lions walked through camp at sun up, stopping to peer into the doorway of the pilots' pup tent. That tent was a bit snug for the two husky men already in it and there was just no room for a lion, let alone two of them. The pilots' cries of alarm alerted George, who was feeding nearby, and seeing the lions at the tent, he screamed and charged, ears outstretched and eyes pink with rage. The lions beat a hasty retreat for the closest bush, and George, after an irritated rumble or two, went back to his feeding. The pilots agreed it would be a good day to do up some laundry.

Since none of us had ever seen an elephant charge a lion except when one got close enough to young elephants to pose a threat to the totos, this action of George's caused no end of speculation and comment from the experts among us.

Another example of George's considerate behavior revolved around the acacia trees. He kept coming back to them about four times each twenty–four hours; half the time with three or four male chums in tow, the rest of the time alone. These trees are sizeable, perhaps seventy feet tall and from two to three feet in diameter at the trunk. The pods are numerous and they ripen and fall over a period of six weeks—but not in regular amounts.

That is to say, there were times when George, with or without friends, would find fewer pods fallen than his hunger would tolerate. On these occasions, a little tree shaking did wonders. This he did by standing on his hind legs, placing his tusks on each side of the tree trunk some sixteen feet above the ground, and pushing rapidly and hard against the tree trunk with tusks and

10•

his own trunk. A few details will bear pointing out.

To shake pods from the top of a seventy–foot tree, considerable pressure must be applied at the shaking point. The shaking can, therefore, be somewhat violent.

When the tree trunk moves violently enough to shake off a pod seventy feet away, it does amazing things to a tent which is tied to the trunk only three feet away.

Apparently aware of these facts, George was considerate enough to shake the trees only in the daytime. We all slept well at night, therefore. There were a few abruptly terminated afternoon naps, of course, with various reactions from the befuddled and shaken arousees, such as, "What the hell, are we having an earthquake?" Other possibilities that came to mind were volcanic eruptions, atomic bombs and collisions with comets. The awakened ones were always mollified, however, when the obvious had been pointed out. Only George's consideration had kept it from happening to them at night.

The good example set for us by George was most salutary in its effect. In only three weeks our own levels of tolerance were nearly on par with his and we became masters at ignoring all sorts of things: among them, leopards and hyenas in camp at night, hippos snorting at the tent door, and snakes in the thatch of the loo's. Our comportment improved to the point that George and his friends were willing to have dinner with us at times— much to the consternation of the Wild Kingdom photography crew that arrived late in our stay and set up their tent nearby.

I suppose it was a bit unnerving to them to look up from their evening cocktails and see four bull elephants' tusks swaying over their heads, gleaming pale silver in the light of the butane lamp. But George and his buddies handled the whole thing with their usual poise and dignity, moving off a few feet to avoid the dust, careful not to step on any of the overturned chairs, pretending not to hear the raucous screams and yelling. It was three nights before they would consider having dinner with us again, however. After all, a person is judged by the company he keeps.

p.

THE HUNTER

The animal was magnificent, a trophy exceeding his wildest hopes. Beautiful coloring in the face, neck and shoulders; majestic, massive horns curving and twisting above, it filled his soul with a mixture of awe and triumph to realize that he had been good enough—lucky enough—to vanquish such an adversary. He walked around it, studying it, mentally estimating the horns. Even as he realized that it would equal, if not actually better the world record, his heart filled with regret. The problem was that the animal was dead.

It was not a matter of regretting his part in that death. It was simply that he wished the animal was still alive, that the affair could have somehow been arranged without its death. It was always this way for him. The time of triumph inevitably was also the time of regret. He admired and respected all wildlife, found the death of any one of them a sad thing. It might well be asked, then, why did he kill any of them if he felt this way?

The answer is simply that he killed because he was a hunter.

For over fifty years he had hunted, beginning at the age of ten. On his twelfth birthday, he traded his BB gun for a single shot twenty–two. At fourteen, he graduated from a 410 shotgun to a sixteen–gauge double. Through the years, the mysteries of animal and bird habits had been solved, until now he could think like his quarry. With increased knowledge came increased respect, and each hunt became a personal contest between himself and the animal, to be fought out under the self–imposed rules he felt were required: fair chase, no shooting from vehicles, no shooting over baits or from blinds; no shooting of young, or female— only old males no longer breeding; no endangered or rare species; no shooting of animals just for his own pleasure, they must be eaten and utilized; no cats, bears, elephants, rhinos, moose, hippo, giraffe, zebra, ostrich, crocodiles—either because he felt they were not truly game animals, or admired them too much to ever hurt one, or because they were such beautiful prehistoric beasts; no more than one record-book animal in any one specie, because that's all a man is entitled to; no animal too small as a trophy to qualify for the record book. This last was the most recent addition to the set of rules within which he permitted himself to hunt. The most important rule of all was that he must always give to wildlife, through his conservation efforts, more than he took. To settle for less, to fudge on his rules, would be to degrade himself; to make of himself a butcher, a game hog, a slob, no longer entitled to the name of hunter.

The rules, coupled with his skill, had combined to create for him some memorable moments—moments which more often than not involved no killing. His most vivid memories were more likely to be of the ones he decided not to shoot, rather than of those he had killed. Because the killing is the least of it, though the rest—and best—of it required the possibility of a kill in order to come to full flower, to season, provide the spice, bring out the full flavor of the experience. It is the knowledge that the kill will occur that makes the ancient primeval brain, the hypothalamus, excite the glands which emit the juices—the chemicals—that raise the level of awareness to heights never realized in life's normal activities. Only the kill expectation can do this. Not the kill itself, not the chase alone. Somehow that primitive brain knows the difference between a gun and a camera.

This hunt would be one that he would savor for whatever years might be left to him. The animal involved, the area in which the hunt had occurred, the degree of difficulty, the world record size—all these factors contributed to a total experience unlike any other.

The animal which he had killed was a Bongo, one

of the larger and more beautiful of Africa's seventy–five species of antelope. It was an exotic trophy, even for Africa, because it was so little known, and among the knowledgeable big game hunters it was considered to be the most difficult trophy in the world. American hunters are inclined to list the mountain sheep as the world's top trophy, but no one who had hunted both sheep and Bongo, as had the hunter, would agree with this. There is no comparison in degree of difficulty between the two.

The hunter had crawled on his belly or on all fours through jungle so thick that a fiery red animal as big as an Angus steer, with eleven white vertical stripes on its sides, in a solid green rain forest, was invisible—*completely* invisible—at distances of ten or fifteen feet. He had tangled with poisonous spiders, caterpillars, and snakes; horrible stinging safari ants; nettles and other stinging plants; fought cut grass ten feet tall that could slice out an eye in one unwary second; swamps waist–deep in muck; oppressive heat and miserable cold rain. With his trackers he had followed tracks of Bongo for miles through this god–awful country, gotten within fifteen feet, heard them crash off through the tangles, and never glimpsed a hair. Day after exhausting day. Good hunters had spent weeks in such arduous quests without success, he knew. He returned to camp late at night feeling that it was hopeless, left at four–thirty each morning determined once more. Every day they found fresh tracks, there were plenty of Bongo in the forests. It was the most difficult challenge of his life, and his admiration for the toughness and intelligence of the animals was unbounded.

It had all paid off, finally, in the trophy lying before him. He hadn't flubbed his chance when it came. A prime old bull, obviously well up in the record book, one good shot opportunity as it fled through a tiny opening. Only when he came up to the bull did he realize that it was a possible world record. Yes, he would remember, relive the moments, feel again the triumph, the accomplishment. But the regret, too—he would feel that as he remembered. He knew all this, standing there.

Later, as he sat in the tiny glade, one small opening in all that endless forest, he had time to think. He was alone now with only the Bongo for company, awaiting the return of the trackers who had gone to drive the car closer. Actually, he was not alone, it's just that there were no other humans there. There were thousands upon thousands of bees, and myriad colorful butterflies —all interested in the blood drying on his shoes and pant legs—as well as dung beetles and birds. He did not feel alone, though the nearest humans were miles away, and damn few of them even there. It was peaceful in the glade, and beautiful—it would become an important part of the memory.

As he sat, he thought of another memorable time,

only two weeks before, and tried to compare the two experiences. That time they had been tracking a herd of eland, largest of the world's antelopes. Eland are very wary, easily spooked and intelligent—hence it is quite difficult to get very close to them. This herd was feeding down a narrow vlei—grassy meadow—between a thick stand of mopane woodland with medium and small–sized trees fairly close together, sparse grass growing between them. The hunter and his tracker cut through the woodland in an effort to get around in front of the eland, and were approaching the edge of the vlei when suddenly they saw an eland feeding toward them just inside the woodland. The men froze, and slowly sat down. To have gone further would have revealed their presence.

The entire herd, some fifty animals, slowly followed the lead of the first one, entering the woodland from the vlei, feeding slowly toward the men. What followed had the slow–motion, ethereal quality of a dream. It was impossible, no way in which it could happen, but it did. The herd came closer and closer, by some miracle not getting the wind of the men, until there were feeding eland within ten, then eight feet of the immobile pair of astonished watchers. Would *nothing* alert the huge beasts? Seemingly, for the pantomime went on for more than twenty minutes. There were two bulls in the herd, but they were young and the horns not of record-book size, so the hunter made no move, only watched. By now there were animals on both sides of them, even a few feet beyond them. They were in the middle of a herd of fifty eland!

An eland cow weighs up to fifteen hundred pounds, a bull can weigh two thousand. When frightened they can out run a horse, or jump a ten–foot fence. They are powerful enough to run right through a chain–link steel fence, the hunter had seen it happen. The thought of the danger that might lie in those thundering hooves if they were to suddenly spook entered the minds of the men, but caused no wavering of their frozen immobility. The thing would be ridden to the end, whatever came—this was a once–in–a–lifetime, or for most a never–in–a–lifetime experience. The animals raised their heads from time to time to stare at the unmoving blobs so close to them. The men were in plain sight, not so much as a blade of grass hiding them. The men were stiff from not moving for so long, when one of the cows detected some movement, and snorted. It was a rather doubtful snort, she was more puzzled than frightened, but it alerted most of the herd. There was a sort of backing off movement, more snorting, but no panic. They actually went back to their feeding again, now some fifty or sixty feet away. Mild snorting continued, and much staring.

"We'll just get up and walk off," the hunter whispered. "Keep an eye out on your backside they don't charge." So off they went, walking noisily through the dry mopane leaves. The eland snorted and stared, but did not run.

The hunter considered; each of the two experiences was a rarity, not likely to happen in a lifetime of hunting. Each in its own way was a rare accomplishment, with its own reward of triumph and gratification. The eland would only exist in his memory, he had no trophy to carry with him. The Bongo would exist as a mounted head—the only one—in his home. He could look at it, take pride in a record, in the top trophy in the hunter's world. It would rekindle the memories, the pride—and the regret. He wondered if the eland weren't somehow the more satisfying.

BOB

All things considered, I could never qualify as a dog lover. Not that I'm a dog hater, it's just that I don't care much about them one way or the other. They all seem to be so doggy, sort of, and that leaves something to be desired in a relationship. We've had a lot of dogs around our house over the years—all sizes, lots of different breeds. They were mostly nice, well–mannered, obedient pets; not a great deal of personality, however. Oh, we had our share of troublesome ones, too—a neurotic springer spaniel that tried to hang itself in the basement, numerous garden despoilers, one three hundred dollar "fully trained" black labrador who jerked the leash from my hand as I was bringing him from the trainer's kennels, ran off and got himself flattened that night on the freeway—that sort of thing, but the majority were good enough, just boring. All except one.

I suppose that a man never owns more than one really great dog in his life; in fact, he's lucky if he manages that, from what I've seen. Mine was called Bob. For twelve years he was my best friend, though the full realization of this fact became clear only after he was gone. During those years he gave me more laughs, more pleasure than anyone except my wife, and some days even she came in second.

As a puppy Bob was no more, and no less, lovable, cute and cuddly than every other puppy I've seen. If they would all *stay* puppies, two or three months old, say, I could become a dog lover in short order. Bob and I sort of trained each other in the early days. I had been hunting ducks for about three years, really didn't know much about it, but did have enough sense to realize I needed a retriever—something to find the birds which fell into the heavy tules we hunted in. Bob was retrieving ducks at the age of six months. I was too ignorant to know that a puppy isn't supposed to do this. We did a lot of things that year that are not supposed to be done—at least not the way we did them. Blissfully unaware, I told Bob to do them, so he did. Much to the astonishment of more knowledgeable hunters and dog–owners.

The thing was that Bob understood English, and that made all the difference. He couldn't speak it, of course. His end of a conversation sounded like the Wookie in Star Wars. One of my hunting companions was very big on Field Trials for retrievers, usually had a dog or two in each one that occurred. One day he

watched Bob retrieve six or seven ducks from a weedy
ten–acre pond. When I came in with my limit, his dog
was off somewhere hunting mice or rabbits, so I asked
Bob to help out—all blind retrieves, since Bob hadn't
been there to see the ducks fall. My friend couldn't
believe it. Most dogs at nine months won't even go out
in a pond if they don't see a bird to go after.

"Go over to your left," I yelled. Bob dutifully
paddled over until he located the bird and brought it in.
The system worked fine for us unless he was so far off
he couldn't hear. I finally had to teach him hand signals
for the really long ones.

He was a large dog, larger than most labs, and very
strong. One day he insisted on going hunting when he
was recovering from an infected shoulder. He retrieved
forty–four ducks for four of us that day—the limit was
eleven in those days—from heavy tules, on three legs.
When healthy, he could jump a five–strand fence with a
fourteen pound honker in his mouth.

He almost met his match one morning, though,
when we were on our way to the blind before daylight.
He disappeared as we passed a large clump of tules, and
right after I noticed his absence a most horrible racket
burst forth from the tules. It went on so long that I was
on the point of going in there myself, when out of the
dark Bob appeared, dragging a most unwilling Sandhill
Crane with him. Not behind him, but *with* him—in fact
all over him. A Sandhill stands four feet high, weighs

twenty–five pounds, and has a seven inch–long beak, sharp as a dagger. It must have been a marvelous battle, from the sounds of it. We turned the bird loose, but he was terribly disgruntled about the whole thing—gave the dog a parting blow with his wing as he stalked off into the darkness.

It was much more than his prowess as a bird–dog, however, that made him so special. In the main, it was his sense of humor. There was the rabbit game he loved to play with me, for instance. Like all dogs, he loved to chase rabbits, which is not a thing to endear a hunting dog to the hearts of those hunters in his party when after pheasants or quail—even ducks. We had several long talks before he decided not to chase any more jack rabbits. He gave up chasing them, but still managed his share of them without in any way fouling up our hunting. This is the way it went:

When we hunted pheasants, Bob coursed through the grass and weeds slightly ahead of me to flush the birds. Every so often there was a jackrabbit in those weeds. Somehow (I never managed to learn how) he was able to "set" most of those rabbits, like a pointer sets a bird. Then, as he worked back and forth, he ran past the hiding animal without breaking stride or slowing down, leaned over and snapped up the rabbit in his jaws. One snap, release, and by the time the rabbit began bouncing up in the air in his death throes, Bob was twenty feet away, not deigning a single glance at the wild kicking, with the damndest innocent "who, me?" look on his face you ever saw.

He had a most unusual method of telling me it was time to stop the car and let him out. He didn't whine, like your average dog. He had more powerful arguments. For some reason, Labradors seem to have considerable gas at times, and he was no exception. In fact, he was worse than most, or maybe what I mean is that his gas was worse than most. When Bob wanted the car stopped, it usually got stopped; I needed the fresh air more than he did.

You may feel that this was sheer coincidence, totally uncontrolled on his part? Not so. It never happened in town, or anywhere that would embarrass either of us. Not in the house, where he spent much of his time, or the office, or the duck clubhouse. But in the open country, when it came time in his mind to eliminate gas, it was either pull over or find a gas mask.

He used this gas warfare for other things. People he didn't like—fortunately there weren't many—would get the treatment. I learned to make sure they weren't in the same car with him. It also worked great for him getting rid of pests. Our clubhouse was an old shack, built up on rickety stilts. Like all old shacks, it was full of mice and rats whose presence was noticeable mostly at night after all were asleep—or trying to be.

One night I had a friend down as my guest who was a bit on the fussy side, and as I was about to drift off I heard him muttering and swearing about the "goddamn rats." It was extremely amusing to hear his expletives, and then the impact of objects being thrown about the room. A final curse as a rat running across his sleeping bag brought him to his feet, the rustling of the bag being picked up, some swearing while he found his shoes, and out he went into the night.

"I'll be damned if I can stand this. I'm gonna go sleep in the car."

I managed to restrain my laughter as he tramped off, indignation spurting from every pore. My son, who was along, asked what the row was about—he'd been asleep through most of it—and I told him.

"Bud didn't like the rats, he's gone to sleep in the station wagon. But not for long," I added.

"Why not?"

"Bob's sleeping in that station wagon."

"Oh yeah—" so we waited, it wasn't long. A tramping up the rickety stairs, an opened door, quickly slammed shut, and more tramping into our room over to his bed. It was pitch dark in there, we couldn't see a thing. We didn't have to.

"Jesus Christ, I couldn't stand it. Even the rats are better than that. Omigod, that damned dog. Even with all the windows open—Jesus Christ, it was cold—that damned dog. I never smelled anything like that before in my whole life."

My son and I almost strangled holding our laughter,

and my son said in a strained voice, "Yeah, we kinda thought you'd be back." Bob liked to sleep alone.

It was not a matter of Bud being a weakling. That dog made a lot of strong men beg for mercy during his lifetime. There are famous winds, like the Santa Ana winds of Southern California, the Williwaws of Alaska, but they pale into insignificance compared to Bob's wind. It could burn a man's eyes, strangle him if he didn't get his head out the window in a hurry. I've had to remove long dead cows that would gag a goat, had to study—far too closely—dead rhino and elephant that were too ripe even for hyena. These were bad, but tepid zephyrs by comparison. An interesting aspect, no pun intended, was that all this was accomplished without a sound. Some fellow travelers were nearly asphyxiated, npi, before they discovered the source of their discomfiture. Needless to say, covert glances in my direction became commonplace, and it was interesting to watch the poorly hidden annoyance turn first to astonishment, then to desperation. As for me, the amusement was worth it.

Bob was actually a very loving, gentle fellow most of the time, but he did have his dislikes. One was skunks. He got the treatment once when he was young, and never forgave them. That one experience taught him that skunks are not to be fooled with, and he never did—fool, that is. He simply made one snap with those massive jaws at the backbone of the skunk before the poor fellow could get his squirter in gear, and it was all over. It worried me a lot at first, because a "skunked" dog is not one of my favorite things, but he never missed, and never smelled of skunk.

Another pet peeve was other dogs growling at him. He never picked a fight, but he never backed away from one either. He retired undefeated; one day he amazed me by soundly thrashing a big Chow and his German Shepherd friend who made the mistake of tackling him in our front yard. There were times, though, when I wished he could be a bit more forgiving; allow maybe two growls, say, before I had to head for a vet to put the growler back together.

And cats. He didn't care much for feral cats. The tabbies of the neighborhood, he couldn't have cared less, simply ignored them. But once we were out of town, any cat we found making it in the wild was fair game. Probably because I shot them when I could— they kill one hell of a lot of birds like quail, ducks and pheasants. In fact, next to crows, who are number one on the list of duck killers, cats rank second—man is third. At any rate, we'd talked it over, and Bob knew I wanted them thinned out so he did his best. Actually, a cat is so damn smart that the wild ones could no more be eliminated than the coyote. We got a few, that's all.

One of them almost got us. Bob was working some tules for pheasant, his 100–pound frame crashing through them like a Mack truck, when an increase in the noise advised me that he had found something. The racket rose to an unprecedented level, and I began to wonder who had found whom. What the hell? Maybe a big feral pig, I thought, a 300–pound boar. It was obvious that the dog was in trouble, I could hear him asking for help. After about five minutes that sounded like sheer pandemonium—snarls, growls, yips, roars— the tules burst apart and out came the damndest, biggest, toughest looking cat I ever saw. Right at me, with Bob in hot pursuit. I hit that cat with a load of highbase sixes at fifteen yards, another load at ten yards, and he kept right on coming. My last shell caught him point–blank at five yards, he rolled, regained his feet and came for me—shaky, but still coming. He died maybe four feet from me, hatred blazing in his eyes until they glazed over.

Christ! Only a cat. But I was shaking, and Bob was doing the dog equivalent of mopping his brow. And what a cat it was! Must have weighed nearly thirty pounds, and the teeth had grown long—over an inch long. That little pussy scared me more than any of the lions I've hunted.

Bob's Wookie–talk said, "Hell, boss, that's enough for one day, let's go home." So we did.

Some of us have had a deer camp in the foothills for over thirty years. During his hunting years, Bob was a member of the group. He came in handy for finding wounded animals, and was the only one in the group who believed my stories. We did some hunting when we ran out of stories, and on one of these occasions were traversing a sidehill that had several large clumps of thick, pin–oak brush on it. Bob smelled something interesting as we passed one of the clumps, and dove into it. As I waited to see what he would run out, there was some cracking and crashing of brush, a sort of coughing grunt, and Bob came out of the clump faster than he went in. He ran straight to me and pressed against my legs, keeping me between him and the brush. The crashing came close, and a medium–sized black bear came out, wheeled when he saw me, and humped his way off into the woods, obviously irritated.

Bob watched him from his perch behind my legs, a mild "woof" his only comment. Afterward he said, "You never told me about *those* mothahs, Boss." I stood reproved.

I suppose it was only natural that his hunting prowess should cause a certain amount of notoriety for Bob. A demand developed for his services at stud. This opened up a whole new world for him, and it was not long until he was tramping after every bitch in heat. To keep him in his kennel at home became a problem, and repairs to the gate were expensive.

We took him to the ranch which was four miles from town. It didn't help much. Whenever the wind was from the north, about half the time, he could smell any bitch that was in. Four miles! I swear to God. It went on for years. He'd be gone all night, come dragging in about eight a.m., lie without moving for five hours in the sun, then gone again that night. Only the hunting was permitted to interfere. Fortunately, it was a small town, and most of the bitches were spayed. His soirees only occurred about three or four times a year.

Of course, there were many legitimate offspring, all legal with papers and fancy names. Quite a few of them turned out to be good hunting dogs. Not great, not like their father. After all, none of them could understand English, or speak Wookie.

THE BONGO

Liz decided to sleep "in" next morning, so Pedro and I had breakfast, picked up Marco, and took off.

"Where are we going this morning?" I asked Pedro. "I notice we're leaving thirty minutes early."

"Going on the west side of the road for a change," he replied. "A local guy I've hunted with before lives over there in the forest, and he usually knows where some big ones are. We'll take him with us today."

We picked up Paul and then John, as usual, went on down the road to where a track took off to the west, turned off and bounced along it for about six miles. When we reached the end of the track, it was still dark, so we sat in the car and snoozed until it started to get light.

"Okay, let's go," Pedro said, and we got out into the mist and started off, following Paul down a faint trail through the grass. The trail went down through a meadow, up the other side, across a corner of the forest, and out on an open mesa, through cultivated patches of manioc, bananas, papayas and melons, to a cluster of thatched huts. I noticed most of them had adobe and wattle walls about four feet up, with thatch above that, and faded paintings on the wall portions. It was a primitive form of art, but quite attractive.

Paul and John called out as we approached the largest of the seven dwellings, for no one was up or about as yet. A small wisp of smoke rose from the fire of the previous night—nothing else moved. Another call from Paul, and an answer from the large hut. In a moment a tall, sleepy fellow came out, pulling on a dirty robe, yawning. He and Paul talked a moment in Shana and then he motioned us over to his recreation hut (thatched roof, no walls) and offered us some stools with hide seats. We sat down and waited while he went back into his hut.

Meanwhile, a scrawny brown dog came over and investigated us, sniffing and then wandering off. I tried to make friends, but he paid no attention to my overtures. Soon the man, whose name was Elias, returned with his sandals on and a nasty looking spear in his hand. He waved at us to follow him and started off down a trail toward the forest. We got up and started after him, with me last in line.

I had taken only two steps when that damned little dog jumped forward and bit me on the left ankle. The wound was not serious, but he did draw blood.

"Now, what the hell?" I thought. The closest anti–rabies serum was in Khartoum, no doubt. No way to check the dog's head for rabies here in the jungle. No planes flying to Khartoum at the moment anyway. And as for killing that dog to check it for rabies, someone else could do it, not me. That dog's owner had a very big spear. I went down the trail and caught up with the others, mentally shrugging my shoulders. Inshallah (if it be the will of Allah).

We walked quietly through the forest until we came to a place where the mesa sloped down into a great meadow.

We turned right and then made our way with some difficulty through half a mile of cut grass that was at least three or four feet over our heads, protecting our eyes. We broke out of the grass at a very large salt lick on the foot of the slope and began to look for tracks. We worked ahead to two more smaller salt licks that were adjuncts of the main one. Nothing fresh. Back to the main lick searching more carefully this time, and there it was. A track, a very big track indeed, and fresh.

Now our problem was which way he went after he left the lick. Checked out the forest ridge, above the lick—nothing. Checked the trails going out into the meadow—nothing. Went up toward the head of the meadow—nothing. Bottom of the meadow—more nothing. Back to the lick.

Just then Paul, who was in the center of the meadow

on the trail, whistled. We gathered around, and looked. The big track again. John and Paul started across the meadow toward the far side, following the tracks. It was tough going. Too much grass beaten down on the trail floor. At the far side we couldn't locate the point where the animal had gone up the ridge and into the forest. Not for maybe fifteen minutes, then John whistled. We gathered again and tracked him up to the top of the low ridge and onto more level ground.

Ha! An oval of crushed grass, colored faintly. He had lain there for a bit, coloring the grass with his sweat, then moved on. We followed. The trail stayed up on the ridge, paralleling the meadow for two miles. The tracking took us more than two hours to follow him that far. Sometimes Marco was able to find the track when we lost it, but more often Paul or John succeeded. God, they were good. John, with his British soldier shoes with no laces, Paul with the extra holes punched in his belt. Almost never did Pedro or I find the track. Much too tough.

We came to a small grove of scattered ironwood trees, half grown. The semi–open area was several hundred feet long, about ninety feet wide. The tracks went along the right side, and so did we, following closely. I saw a clump of brush on the left side ahead of us. There was something, just a blur, of orange–red in that brush. Could it be?—no, couldn't be; must be a termite mound, though there weren't many in the forest.

The trackers were ahead of me, they would have seen it.

We went on, coming up ninety degrees from the brush clump. Paul stopped suddenly, raised his hand. We all froze, hardly breathing. He pointed to the clump of brush. I could see nothing there now—only green. Pedro studied the brush with his glasses. And studied, saying nothing. We all stood, silent, unmoving. Several times Pedro took the glasses down to rest his eyes, then back again to look some more. Maybe three, four minutes we stood there. Seemed much longer. Finally, he nodded, grabbed my arm and whispered, "See the clump of brush, there is a bongo in there. Shoot him."

"I can't see a damn thing but brush," I whispered, looking through my scope.

I looked at the brush with my naked eye, could see a shadow in the middle—no color, no form, only a shadow. I looked again through my scope; no shadow, the scope couldn't resolve anything that far back into the brush.

"I can't see a damn thing," I repeated softly.

"Shoot anyway," Pedro whispered.

I aimed where I thought I had seen the shadow and fired. As I slid the second round, a solid, into the chamber I heard Pedro shouting, "He's up—he's coming out, get ready."

The bongo came staggering out of the brush in a lurching run and I thought he was hard hit. I fired again, taking just a hair too little care with the shot. He hunched, I knew I'd hit him behind the shoulder, but maybe just a bit too far behind—? Anyway, he started to run full out, ran behind a huge windfall of logs and limbs, and into the solid wall of forest.

"Piga, piga," Marco cried.

"He's hit all right," Pedro said. "Let's go after him."

As we hurried to the point where he'd entered the thick stuff, John came up holding a leaf with blood on it. I noticed that mixed in with the blood was some rough matter—half digested stuff. Damn. Too far back. And the bullet had been a solid. Must have gone clear through him. The shot would kill him, but not for an hour—maybe even two. We could lose him easily in that time, unless the blood trail held up, and the solid would have made small holes. Damn.

We found more blood and started after the bongo, as fast as we could. There was a fair amount of blood, and the tracking was relatively easy for about a half mile. We found where he had stopped, laid down, then gone on. Then the blood trail started drying up, and we were forced to track him between drops that were further and further apart. Suddenly a crash, not more than ten feet from us, on our left. The track was straight, but he had circled and was watching his back track. He did not charge, but bolted off again. We did not see so much as a red hair, the bush was a solid wall.

We found where he had lain a second time. More blood. The trail was fresher once more as the bleeding started again from his running. The trail went on and on. Through vines and thickets, windfalls and brush piles, and finally out into the half and half zone of part meadow and part forest. No more blood now, not for over a quarter of a mile. My God, I thought, we are going to lose him, and leave him to die out there. I hated the thought. It was obvious that Pedro was thinking much the same thing, as he muttered grimly, "I'm going to follow that son–of–a–bitch until we get him, if it takes 'til sundown."

But time after time we would lose the track, all of us wandering in ever larger circles in the waist–high grass until someone would whistle, and we would be back on the track again. I gave up trying to admire those trackers enough—they were beyond belief. Even Elias helped, carrying his spear much more carefully now.

"Be careful if you see him, Jack," Pedro said. "Bongo are very dangerous when they are wounded. Nearly as dangerous as buffalo. This is a big one, about twenty–nine inches."

At least two miles from where I'd shot him, and about two hours after, the trackers stopped and suddenly pointed to a patch of thick stuff dead ahead, not over thirty–five feet in front of us. They almost went crazy because we didn't shoot. But neither Pedro nor I could see what they saw, try as we might. The bongo jumped out the far side of the copse, and bounded off on Pedro's side—I saw one flash, that's all —and Pedro got one shot. He was obviously pretty badly wounded or he wouldn't have allowed us to get that close, and Pedro's shot broke a front leg. This didn't slow him noticeably, but the new wound bled profusely, and I knew that we had him now.

We followed him to another bunch of heavy brush. This time we could partially see him, and I fired into his chest. He did not drop, so I tried to make out his neck (not an easy task, looking toward the sun with all that brush between us) and shot my last shell at what I hoped was his neck. I missed, because he ran again, and Pedro fired twice more, snap shots that also seemed to miss.

"You'll have to finish him, Pedro," I said, "I'm out of shells." It had never occurred to me that it would be possible to get that many shots in such thick brush, and I'd left the extra rounds in camp. I felt terribly foolish, as the bongo went down, got up, went down, got up again. He was refusing to die, tough as a buffalo. Pedro shot him again with his 458, full in the shoulder. He was staggering on his feet. I said, "Finish him, for God's sake."

It was Pedro's turn to look sheepish. "I'm out of shells, too."

"Good Lord, send that guy with the spear in there, then. We can't just stand here and let him suffer."

"And get Elias killed? No way. Anyhow, he wouldn't go near that bongo, he knows how dangerous they are."

So we stood, helpless, like the numbskulls we were, and watched the gallant bull die on his feet, falling on his side like some great oak, finally, with a crash of brush. It took maybe three minutes, but seemed a very long while to one ashamed hunter and his professional.

At the crash of his final fall, a great cheering went up from all four trackers and we hurried forward through the brush to where he lay on his side.

"My God, look at that bongo," said Pedro softly, a note of hushed awe in his voice. "He is the biggest I have ever seen."

"Oh, wow, what a beauty," understatement of the year from yours truly.

The trackers were touching him, his huge horns, his glossy red coat, with white stripes up and down, talking and laughing all at once, clapping each other on the back in congratulations. I was in a daze, as they came up grinning widely, to solemnly shake my hand, each in turn.

"Pedro," I said, "I think you were wrong about how big he is. Those horns are more than twenty–nine inches."

"Oh, right, right, I was wrong. He is bigger than my big one of thirty–two and a half, even. His horns are bigger, and his size is bigger—bigger than any bongo in Africa this year, and maybe last year, too. My God, I can't believe him—no wonder he was so tough to kill, he is a monster."

Pedro turned to me and took my hand, and I swear he brushed away a tear of happiness as he said, "I am so happy that we got him for *you*, Jack. Of all my hunters, you are the one who should have this great bongo."

I was touched, speechless. I could not say all that was in my heart. I could only say inadequately, "Thank you, Pedro." I hope he knew some of what I was leaving unsaid.

It was several minutes before our euphoria subsided and we began discussing more practical matters, like how to get to the car, or vice versa. There was also a matter of pictures. We had no camera equipment with us, of course. When you hunt in the rain forest you take only what is really necessary. Getting through that stuff is tough enough without dragging along anything extra.

"We'll leave him in this shade here, which will last all day," Pedro said. "I must go for the car and see how close I can get—I do not think I can make it all the way."

He discussed the matter with the trackers. They agreed that to get the car any closer than where we had parked that morning would be impossible. Could it have been only five and a half hours ago?

"We must go to camp for the camera. We want pictures before he is skinned."

"Can you pick up Liz and bring her back with you?" I asked. "I'd like her to see him before we cut him up."

"You bet. What equipment shall I tell her to bring?"

"The small movie camera, the 35mm, two rolls of movie film, and the Polaroid and two packs of film for it. She knows where everything is. I'll gut him and cool him while you are gone so he won't spoil."

"Good idea. I'll leave Marco to help you. We'll be quite a while getting back here. It's almost an hour drive to camp, after we get the car."

"We'll be okay," I said. "Don't worry about us."

Pedro, Elias with his spear, John and Paul started for the car without further delay. It was already eleven–thirty, and picture taking would be impossible after about four–thirty. Fortunately, the bongo had gone down at the edge of a tiny glade, perhaps thirty feet across, and I could get pictures there. Most of the forest was far too dense for successful photography. I was lucky.

I got out my penknife and started working on the bongo. Marco looked askance, my knife so small, but I have been using one like this for thirty–five years, cleaning deer, elk, coyotes, etc., and was not concerned. Anyway, I had no other. (I have always thought the big bladed sheath knives worn on the belt by so many hunters were pretty ostentatious, and am too lazy to pack around all that unnecessary weight.)

The cleaning went well, though we had a good deal of difficulty rolling him, he was so heavy. I have raised cattle, and am used to judging the weight of steer and heifers on the hoof. This bongo weighed close to eight hundred pounds, I'm sure. The weight of an average bongo bull is about six hundred pounds, so Pedro's astonishment in seeing him close up was quite understandable.

We finished the job, covered him with branches, and sat down in the shade to wait. A half hour since Pedro and the others left; I figured it would be four p.m. before they got back, so we had four hours to wait. We made ourselves comfortable seats on the ground with boughs and sat leaning against some young trees, looking forward to a well needed rest, perhaps a nap.

No way. Though Marco was soon snoring, I couldn't sleep. There were three zillion bees buzzing around us. I rose to cover the bongo more completely to keep out the flies and bees, and settled down once again to contemplate my navel. The bees were not "killer bees," but the meat eaters some call yellowjackets in the U.S. They were happily crawling all over my shoes, socks and pant legs where drops of blood had spattered. I finally decided they weren't going to sting me and let them crawl. That way, I figured, the ones that were on me would keep the others off. Worked out fine, I wasn't bitten or stung once.

By now, hundreds and hundreds of butterflies had gathered. Four different types—very pretty and fun to watch. They also were interested in the blood, which surprised me.

Four different dung beetles plied their trade within a few feet of me, and this I had always found highly entertaining. The beetles collect balls of dung bigger than themselves (some the size of pinpong balls) and roll them across the ground to some select spot where, after laying their eggs in the ball, they bury them. The larvae, when hatched, live on the dung, and the ground is aerated, fertilized, and filled with humus. The beetles push the balls with their hind feet, traveling backwards and upside down, and it's really amazing what obstacles they are able to navigate around, over or under; they are so incredibly strong. Every now and then a second beetle will attempt to steal the dung ball, and while the owner and hijacker argue it out, quite often a third will sneak in and make off with it, unnoticed by the two combatants.

It was a delightful way to spend a few hours, I was not at all lonesome, even with Marco asleep. Plenty of birds to watch, the drone of the insects made pleasant background music, and I was really alone. Miles from even primitive civilization, in beautiful lush green surroundings, a floor show entertained me—what more could one ask? No vultures in the rain forest, I noticed. Must be too thick for them to spot food. I looked at Marco, sound asleep. He appeared much older than his twenty years, like most Africans. A sudden frightening thought struck me, "What if a leopard winds the bongo and comes to it? Or lion, hyenas? No shells for the gun." Not even a spear, my defenses consisted of one small penknife.

But it was too peaceful to worry long. I thrust the momentary thought from my mind and went back to the floor show. It was one of the most beautiful spots I've ever seen, that little bosky glade.

I thought about Pedro's reaction to the bongo. When we managed an unusually good animal, usually he was excited, shouting in both Portuguese and English and waving his arms; the bongo had evoked a much different mood, one of reverence, almost. The animal must have had some kind of mystique for him, I thought, or perhaps the sheer magnificence of it was a bit overwhelming.

So passed the afternoon, and I was content. A rare interlude of quiet contemplation, far from the pain and troubles of the modern world. I felt richer than Midas.

NO PROBLEM, MADAME, SHOOT THE LION!

Arturo could, by no stretch of the imagination, be considered an average type of professional hunter. Among a group noteworthy for unique individualism, he stood out head, shoulders and land rover. Some generalizations can be made about professional hunters despite their rugged refusal to be typed, but few of these would apply to Arturo. Most professionals are friendly: Arturo felt that a reply to "good morning" was a waste of his time. The normal professional likes animals: Arturo hated them. Most professionals make an effort to please their client: Arturo either ignored or growled at his. For many reasons he was called "Turo" to his face and "the Stone" behind his back. He ran the safari camp at Gemeiza in Southern Sudan.

It was a large camp, hunting up to sixteen clients at a time, sprawling carelessly on the banks of the White Nile alongside a Shilluk village. The area was stiff with game so there was a good bit of killing done each day, and since Turo had thoughtfully located the skinning tents right next to the camp roundavels, there were no end of flies, kites, and vultures about at all times. The temperature would have been one hundred and twenty–five degrees in the shade, had there been any. All in all, the camp was a place where one could really appreciate a convivial host—had there been any.

Turo had worked out a splendid arrangement with the Shilluk in the village. The camp kept them supplied with meat, in return for which the natives beat very noisily on many large drums all night long. The arrangement was ideal. The roundavels had no screens on the windows. The incessant throbbing drums kept the flies (and everything else) awake all night so there was no danger of any windows being inadvertently left open and clients catching a chill when the nighttime temperature fell to one hundred and ten.

In spite of this cooperation from the Shilluk, Turo hated them as much as he hated everyone else, a fanaticism which caused considerable inconvenience at times. The camp crew—cooks, waiters, and such—were Shilluks and therefore, to Turo, all thieves, not to be trusted. He locked everything up during the day when he was out in the bush hunting with his clients. That could be from sun–up to two in the afternoon, sometimes later.

The camp's water came from the Nile, and though

this branch of the river was called the "white", it looked more like chocolate. If the water hadn't been filtered, you would have to chew it before swallowing. One could get mighty thirsty before tackling any of it in its natural state. All this meant that clients returned hot, tired and thirsty from the hunt, then sat around awaiting Turo's return and regaled each other with recollections of how great that ice water had tasted before Turo locked it all up and took the key with him, which they did every day, because he did, every day.

Most people whose work brings them into frequent contact with wild animals have a well–developed sense of respect and affection for them. Not so our hero. He had all the respect and affection for them that the average human feels for a biting mosquito. All this did not endear Turo to the other professional hunters in the camp, most especially Luis Pedro.

The conflict started when they opened the camp for the season. Turo, Luis Pedro, and John—another professional—had gone out to shoot some tiang for camp rations. John had worked with Turo for several years and was used to his cruelty, but for Luis Pedro this was his first experience. They located some of the purple–red, hartebeest–type antelopes without any trouble and stopped the pickup. Each man picked out an animal and fired. Two taing fell dead at the shot, but one ran off, hard hit, into a copse of heavy brush. Luis Pedro prepared to follow the track of the wounded animal into the bush to finish it. Before he could, Turo set fire to the brush.

"What the hell are you doing?" Luis yelled.

"Ha, he does not get away from the fire," Turo grinned.

"But we could have gotten him easily," Luis protested. "Now he is ruined, and he will suffer needlessly."

"My Shilluk like their meat roasted." A wicked smirk mocked Luis and proclaimed Turo's compassion.

"Forget it," John advised Luis. "It is Turo's way; you will not change him if you talk until Christmas."

A few days later Luis gritted his teeth as he watched Turo's handling of a reedbuck hunt. The client made a very poor shot, breaking both the gazelle's hind legs. Turo drove his pickup to the struggling animal where, instead of killing it, he picked it up and threw it in back. As Turo drove off to continue his hunt, Luis, unbelieving, rubbed his curly hair and wondered how long that wretched reedbuck would lie suffering in the broiling sun. When he returned to camp from his hunt, he found out.

"Luis, come here," Turo hailed him. "See what we have got this morning." He pointed proudly to a yellow–maned lion lying dead in the bed of his pickup. Luis casually inspected the lion, which was only an average specimen. He noticed a reedbuck lying under the lion. Startled, he gave it a second glance. It had moved slightly.

"For God's sake, Turo! That reedbuck is still alive. Why don't you kill it?"

"It goes nowhere," Turo glared at him, "and it skins easier if it's still warm."

"Damn you, kill that reedbuck *now*, or I will."

Turo hesitated, shrugged, and ordered his skinner to cut the reedbuck's throat. From this time, Luis Pedro referred to Turo as "the Stone," and the name stuck.

Turo smoked cigars constantly, even while hunting. The habit nearly cost him his life. He and Luis Pedro were hunting with an English couple, the wife with Turo in his land rover. For convenience and because he felt no compunction to follow the usual rules of "fair chase" in his quest for game, the cab and windscreens of the land rover had been removed to permit shooting from the car. The clients were old hands in the bush and the wife very particular about killing her own trophies without any help from hubby. The two cars kept within shooting distance of each other as they hunted.

Reedbuck were everywhere, and it was not long before Turo pointed out a good ram to the woman and urged that she shoot it—which she did, while seated in the land rover. Forgetting the ever present cigar in his fingers, Turo gave her a congratulatory slap on the back as the animal dropped. The lady's indignation at Turo's unexpected familiarity rapidly gave way to pained discomfort as a shower of hot ashes fell down inside the back of her shirt.

At this moment, a large male lion charged them head on from some bushes behind the fallen ram. Turo's gun was in the back with the tracker. "No problem, Madame, Shoot the lion," Turo yelled.

The lion was coming in long, low bounds with incredible speed, its slobbering mouth agape and roaring rage.

"No *problem*, Madame! *Shoot the lion*!" Turo yelled desperately.

The good lady, wrestling with her shirt, trying to get the burning ashes off her back, was in no mood or position to shoot anything. It became utter pandemonium. In desperation Turo leaped from his side of the car. The lion switched to the moving target, cleared the rover's hood in one snarling leap, and hit Turo in the back.

By this time the two men in the other car had realized the danger and sprung into action. Luis Pedro, moving quickly, arrived with his rifle to blow the lion off the sprawling Turo, who was screaming loudly for help. The lady, meanwhile, had managed to bail out of the rover, get the singed shirt off, and beat out the final glowing sparks. Without stopping to replace the shirt, with determined stride, she rounded the rover and came up to her grimacing, mauled professional, now crawling out from under the lion.

"You idiot! You stupid, blithering idiot! If you ever

dare touch me again, I'll fix you so that you will think that lion was a pussy cat. Now stop your moaning and get us back to camp. I need a new shirt."

On the way to camp her husband asked Luis, "Why did you hesitate just before you shot that lion? I didn't just imagine it, did I?"

"Nope. Just wanted to give him one more bite of that damned Turo." A happy grin spread over Luis' face, and he began to whistle quietly.

THE FERTILIZER COMPANY

Sometimes the end result of an action cannot be foretold by even the most careful planning, or the most able of seers. Perhaps this is a good thing, else there might be precious little action taken in this mixed–up world. Be that as it may, once begun, things have a way of moving under their own power, one thing leading to another, with each leap gaining momentum until the very devil himself would be troubled to undo the tangle and set the action to rest. The fertilizer company was a case in point.

It began with, of all things, our retail butane distributorship. In our areas, summer temperatures reach one hundred fifteen, and average around ninety–five degrees. Our customers, encouraged by such warmth, showed a certain lack of enthusiasm for our product during these months, and we found ourselves stumbling over Joe, our one and only truck driver. Any fool could see that paying someone to keep getting underfoot wasn't too efficient, so my partner, George, suggested we might look for a sideline that would peak in the summertime and give Joe something to do. A moderately intensive search produced what seemed at the time the ideal solution—the liquid fertilizer business.

It was summer–intensive, and our area was primarily agricultural. Liquid fertilizer was a totally new concept—we became the second company in California to manufacture liquid fertilizers—and it involved the use of a liquid gas, ammonia, held under pressure in tanks like our usual products, butane and propane. Ideal, right? Wrong.

We did keep Joe busy all summer, but the side–effects were little short of cataclysmic. Come to think of it, we did more than keep Joe busy. He ended up averaging about seventy–two hours of work each week. Not to mention the new sales manager, warehouseman, mechanic, and two *more* truck drivers who had to be hired, and the countless hours worked by the partners themselves. Our little two–man butane operation had grown a sizeable tail, and was getting one hell of a wagging from it.

Before we knew quite what had happened to us, we had nine dealerships in surrounding areas, a plant manufacturing night and day, dozens of storage tanks, trailers, applicators scattered all over Northern California—and we were borrowed up to the limit at the bank.

We also none of us knew what the hell we were

doing, none of us. Especially me. I knew, more or less, what the others were doing, even if they didn't, because I was the one who had *told* them what to do. The problem was that I didn't know what *I* was doing, so that meant that none of us, really, knew what he was doing. We were doing one God–awful lot of it, though, whatever it was. We did it all day, half the night, and Sundays and holidays. Farmers, at least some of them, work all the time—so did we.

Except in winter. We repaired equipment in winter, and tried to collect money to keep operating. Joe went back to driving a butane truck in winter. My partner asked each winter if we had made any money, in the fertilizer business, that is. I kept telling him, "Don't worry. We found something for Joe to do in the summer."

One winter the rains came early, and all the bean growers failed to harvest their beans. They couldn't pay us, so by spring we were all working without salaries, and down to the last few hundred dollars in the till. Somehow we made it through. It made no real difference; going down the tubes or crawling back up—we didn't know what the hell we were doing either direction.

It became a way of life. When you don't know any better, you can do anything, because you don't know it can't be done. Some experts may tell you it can't be done, but you don't know for sure, so you go ahead and do it—especially if there's no other way.

Our three big 30,000 gallon storage tanks were installed—as per the engineer's instructions—on foot thick cement slabs, reinforced with pig–wire fencing, on top of eighteen inches of gravel. Only one thing the engineer forgot; to check out the ground beneath the gravel. During our second year all the slabs cracked across the middle, both directions, and sank about a foot or more in the center. The cracks went completely through the slabs from top to bottom, so that only the wire reinforcement was holding them. It was summer, we couldn't stop operating long enough to empty the tanks or we'd be bankrupt. Those slabs had to be fixed while the tanks were full.

Four different engineers came and studied our problems and all of them had the identical opinion: "It can't be done." No suggestions, no possibilities to explore, nothing. So we fixed the slabs the only way I could think of, the way they said couldn't work.

Two four–foot deep trenches ten feet long were dug on opposite sides of each slab. A trench in the center was dug under the slab in the center to connect the first two. One man at a time worked in that center trench; it was just big enough to hold him lying on his side, chipping away with a pick that had a one–foot handle. We kept a rope tied to his ankles, just in case my esti- mate of the strength left in that wire in the broken slab wasn't so hot. We put a 16 foot H–beam bridge girder in the center trench, with six–foot square steel plates welded top and bottom, jacked it up against the slab bottom, pushed the whole thing up four inches above level, then poured cement in all three trenches until they were full. We pulled the man out of the trench first.

Those slabs never moved after that. The plant was eventually sold and moved to another location. The slabs are still there, though a D–9 dozer spent a day trying to move them. We found when we dug the trenches that our tanks had been installed over a sixty–year old garbage dump. Looking back on it, I think the four engineers were probably right.

Everything we did was improvised, because no one else had ever done any liquid fertilizing before. Liquids were brand new. We had to invent and build most of our own applicators. The experts told us that our fertilizers wouldn't work for rice. Today all California rice is fertilized by liquids, using applicators built with our original designs.

I didn't *always* know what the others were doing, of course. Some of our men were pretty good improvisors themselves. The tanks suffered from corrosion and rust, and it was necessary to repaint them each year. The smaller tanks presented no problem, but the big tanks were over thirty feet tall. Two of the fellows were assigned the job of painting them. They finished the part they could reach from the ground on ladders, then went up on top and painted down as much as they could reach. I went to borrow some scaffolding, returned to find they had rigged a rope and pulley system, with a bos'n's chair.

They were raising—and lowering—the chair by means of a rope tied to the rear bumper of their car. My hair turned several shades grayer as I watched. The painter would sit in the flimsy chair, hang onto the rope sides for dear life, and his partner driving the car would start off, car wheels spinning gravel like a dragster. The painter found himself jerked thirty feet up the tank in less than a second. They had been using the system for several hours, taking turns. With each turn the new driver would "get even" for his previous ride in the chair, so that by the time I arrived the chair rider was damn near going into orbit. Certain modifications in the system were instituted shortly after my arrival. The only casualty was the spilled paint.

The stuff we were playing around with was a far cry from horse manure. The chemicals we mixed and applied every day could kill damn quick if anyone got careless with them. Even with all our precautions some interesting moments occurred and some even involved customers, who were always curious about the "new–fangled" equipment and chemicals.

We were setting up a water flow application, one in which the ammonia is metered through a hose from a small tank into an open ditch of irrigation water. The farmer was watching the activities with great interest, and when the hose carrying the aqua—water and ammonia mixed—from the tank to the ditch was placed in the ditch water, he reached down suddenly and picked it up.

Before any of us could move, he put the end of the hose to his face and took a healthy sniff. His mouth went slack, his eyes glazed, and he fell flat on his face, stiff as a board. I almost died, and was sure he *had*.

We rolled him over, saw his eyes were wide open, but he wasn't breathing. A long, shuddering breath finally shook his chest, and moments later he was back on his feet, breathing normally. The concentrated ammonia gas he'd inhaled had paralyzed his diaphragm muscles, and he'd blacked out. His suspicions that we might be selling him plain water had been allayed the hard way.

The fact that there were a bunch of half–crazy neophytes flying blind around the northern part of the state was common knowledge, I suppose, because we began to be approached by dozens of kooks and con–artists. We were urged to buy every kind of magic elixir and potion ever conceived, all absolutely guaranteed to grow bumper crops on billiard balls.

One night, along with some of my competitors from around the state, I attended a meeting where we received the weirdest sales talk I ever heard. The product was called Bio–something or other, made from the rumen of pregnant cows, and contained—supposedly

—bacteria from said rumen. It would turn hardpan into lush loam, cure all water–penetration problems, and even, we were solemnly assured, cure completely any sores from radioactivity in case of nuclear war. "Just rub it on," the salesman said.

The weirdest part of all was that it was supposed to be delivered to the dealer—us—in concentrate form. Add eight thousand gallons of water to 2,000 gallons of concentrate, wait seventy–two hours for the bacteria to proliferate, and presto kazaam! Ten thousand gallons of miracle water. I couldn't resist that one; ordered the two thousand of concentrate delivered. We tried it quite a few places where nothing else would work—ground too poor—with a complete spectrum of results. If you could believe the farmers, that is. All the way from fantastic to zilch.

From my own observations, I could believe the zilch ones with little difficulty. Unfortunately, I never ran into a victim of a nuclear bomb, so that aspect of the miracle liquid was never checked out. We never sold any of it, just gave it away as "experimental." It was a great way to make friends, we found.

We also discovered that bacteria from cow rumens can't count. Every time our ten thousand gallons got down to two thousand, we just added eight thousand gallons more water right back into the tank, and the little buggers proliferated all over again. Never had to order another load of concentrate. We were pretty sure they proliferated, at any rate—never could actually see one of them, even in the original load—we figured they would have to be doing *something* in all that nice warm water.

The fertilizer company operated for six years, though it seemed more like a lifetime. We had to sell out to a major oil company after they got into the business. When Shell, Union and Chevron start a price war with each other, the little local guys become expendable, rapidly. It was fun while it lasted, and we all learned a lot. We did things that were impossible, things that were stupid, things that were dangerous. They were exciting, a lot of them; interesting, most of them; boring, none of them. One of them was the funniest thing that has ever happened to me—even today thinking about it can make me laugh until tears come.

It started with one of the countless salesmen who were always pushing a new miracle additive on us, or trying to. I'd seen a hundred like him before, and was busy preparing a pleasant "Thanks a lot, but no thanks" for him when he performed his demonstration. It stopped me speechless, though it was simplicity itself. He filled a Dixie cup with water, held it up and put two drops of his stuff in the cup with an eye dropper. The water, to my complete amazement, immediately leaked right through the cup and all over the floor.

To say that I was impressed is the understatement of the year. Anything that could increase the permeability of soils would make our fertilizers work twice as well, of course, so I couldn't wait to order a load of the mysterious chemical. It was delivered in due time, and we immediately decided to add some to one of the delivery trucks that had just finished loading a tankful of aqua ammonia and was on the point of pulling out of the yard to make a delivery.

The driver looked somewhat askance when I handed him a gallon jug of the dark brown liquid, but we were always trying something new so he merely shrugged and asked how much to put in. This was a problem, since the stuff came with no instructions, but the truck's tank held fifteen–hundred gallons, so I told him to try just one gallon this first time. He poured it in the top of the tank and started off to the farmer's, where the aqua would be pumped into a field–storage tank. I jumped in my car and passed him on my way to locate the customer and alert him to the pending arrival of our new improved aqua.

Everything was quite normal, apparently. I drove the five miles to town, through it and on another five miles to the farm where I found the farmer out in the field applying fertilizer. I waited at the storage tank for a few minutes, until he brought the applicator in for a refill. We had barely exchanged pleasantries when my driver drove up with the truck.

I started to help, stuck the truck's fill hose in the storage tank, noticed an extremely harried look on the driver's face, and wondered vaguely about the wetness on the sides of the truck tank. I told the driver to start the pump.

"I dunno boss," he said. Surprised, I looked up and told him again. He raised his eyebrows in a "here we go again" manner and gave the starter a pull. The pump chattered to life, and all hell broke loose. Huge billowing masses of foamy bubbles came pouring from every open orifice in the truck tank. Beautiful, huge bubbles. They poured onto the ground and spread in all directions, two feet deep. On and on they poured forth, an endless cascade of froth and foam. And inside all those bubbles was ammonia fumes, not just air. It was a sight to make strong men blanche, and a smell to make anything living wish it was somewhere else—fast!

I made a dash for the farmer, who was standing to one side, paralyzed by the sheer magnitude of the whole scene. As I grabbed his hand to pull him upwind, he said,

"Good God Almighty! What in hell *is* that stuff?"

He got no answer from me. I wasn't sure myself. The driver had walked upwind when the pump started, and was watching the torrents pouring forth with unconcealed awe. Reaching clear air, I turned to stare—and stare. Words failed me. I looked at the farmer, who was staring unbelieving at the spectacle, muttering "good God Almighty" at each new burst of bubbles that spurted into the air. It was magnificent. I began to laugh—and laugh. The other two turned to stare at me, then joined in. We howled, ran out of breath, sat down on the ground and laughed 'til we cried.

The tank finally empty, we managed to get the pump turned off and looked at the storage tank. It was less than half full. The farmer, still chuckling said, "I ain't payin' for no full tank of whatever in hell that was, or is."

"This one's on us, Joe. You'll lose a bunch more trying to fill your applicator, probably."

"Christ, I forgot about that. It won't explode, will it?"

"No, it's just a new additive we put in to help the aqua penetrate further and better. It's highly concentrated detergent, breaks down the surface tension of any liquid it's mixed with. We just put too much in."

"Wish Ma coulda been here to see it. Gawd, wasn't it somethin'?"

Later the driver told me the rest of the story. The magic formula had undergone a good bit of jiggling by the time he reached town, and the first intimation he'd had of any problem was the excited waving and pointing of pedestrians as he drove down the main street. Looking back, he was horrified to see the truck tank top and sides completely hidden in bubbles, and huge frothy chunks of foam breaking off and flying in all directions. A highway patrolman pulled him over in the center of town, demanding, "What in hell's name is that stuff you are spraying all over the street?"

As the driver started to explain—though he didn't really know what was going on himself—the ammonia fumes began to gag the patrolman, who coughed, choked and yelled, "Never mind. Just get that truck the hell out of here. Christ!" Forgetting all dignity, he bolted for the patrol car, got in, and rolled up the windows.

The frothing had quieted down by the time the truck reached the farm, only to be renewed with increased vigor by the starting of the pump. We had to cut down the mixture to two ounces for each tanker load before we could stop the foaming. I never saw that salesman again, and was unable to locate any source for his amazing product, so we used up the first shipment and that was the end of it. All things considered, that was pretty much the story of the Fertilizer Company.

KEFUNDI, THE GRYSBOK

"Jambo, Bwana." John, the tracker, was smiling, his white teeth gleaming in the torch light against his chocolate brown face.

"Jambo, John." I returned his smile and asked, "Well, what are we going to hunt today?"

"Ah, one must not talk of the animal we will hunt, Bwana. It is very bad luck to mention him, and you will not shoot him if I say his name."

"You mean I can't talk about the trophy I want? How will Luis Pedro know which animal it is?" This was the first I'd heard of such a superstition among the blacks.

"It matters not if you and the Sahib Pedro talk of it, Bwana. Only if we do." A wave of his hand included the skinner and the mechanic, the other two black members of the crew sitting with him in the back of the land rover pickup.

I stowed the cameras and binoculars on the seat, the

box of ammo in the glove compartment, and climbed in. Luis Pedro walked up, looked back, quickly checking to make sure the lunch box, winch, and jerry cans had been loaded. He joked briefly with the crew in Bembe and climbed in behind the wheel.

"All set?" he asked, starting the engine and turning on the headlights.

"Yep."

We took the road that went up through the savannah plains along the river. It was cold, and I hunched down into the down jacket. Tired of staring at the winding wheel tracks being swallowed and spit out by the headlights, I mentioned to Pedro the superstition that John had expressed to me.

"Yes, they all believe that." Pedro laughed. "You should hear them when they don't like one of my clients. They talk about every animal on the license."

"Not that I don't take it seriously," I chuckled. "But it's a new one to me. I hear new beliefs every time I come to Africa. Do you believe that every animal has a 'time,' Pedro? You know, a time when it's *supposed* to die?"

"Sure, people too. Everything has its time. When its 'time' you do what's necessary to get yourself killed. Animals do that all the time. Or at least they don't do anything to try to avoid death."

We rode in silence awhile; that was pretty heavy stuff, especially with Pedro driving over the twisting track like a maniac. He had this theory that if you went fast enough you didn't feel the bumps. I thought, "according to his idea about one's 'time,' the fact that I am willing to ride in a car with him driving is an invitation to the grim reaper," and shivered a bit. It sure was cold. False light was showing, you could see beyond the headlights. Pretty soon Pedro turned them off. Dawn was breaking off to the right over the bush.

This is a special time in Africa. The dew glistens in silver mottlings across the grass, and the little ground mist rises everywhere in the greyness, and all the colors begin to materialize out of that same greyness so gradually that you don't see the change until you realize it already *has*. The shadows turn into shapes, and the shapes become trees and bushes and termite mounds. Then, after fifteen or twenty minutes of it that leaves you thinking you've never seen anything more beautiful, the real show starts. The sun comes up, and the puffy cumulus clouds go from purple to pink to light orange to yellow and finally back to white as the sky across the world from the sun turns blue, and everything gets sharp—clear and distinct—so sharp that it hurts your eyes a little to look at it. Suddenly you notice some different shapes that are moving. They are female hartebeest with young trotting at their heels, or perhaps a pair of lions returning to the heavier bush from the night's feeding, or if you're really lucky, a leopard crossing the road, belly swinging low to the ground.

You feel the electric thrill of the chase start up your spine and realize you're in Africa, in the real bush, and life is so full, so full you can hardly stand it without crying out. This is not a time for talking. It is a time for being—for being alive, and for being *there.*

With the coming of light, Pedro stopped driving like a madman, and we were happy to just idle along enjoying ourselves. We stopped the car a half a mile short of a salt lick to make a sneak, hoping for a chance at an eland – the only trophy I was interested in. No dice. We were too late or too noisy, and the lick was deserted. We found plenty of tracks, some quite fresh, and decided to follow them up. An eland's normal walking speed— even with the constant feeding—is about five miles an hour. He is also as smart as any wild animal in the bush and watches his back trail constantly. You can count on a lot of walking when you track an eland. The finding can be very scarce or nonexistent.

We never saw these eland, eventually losing them where they were jumped by lions and scattered in all directions. We gave up then. Walking eland are tough; running eland are impossible. They might keep running for twenty miles.

But we were not bored, in spite of our failure. We flushed bushbuck, oribi, and grysbok out of the combiatum ahead of us; saw a small herd of nine roan; were saved from walking right into a lioness and two half-grown cubs only by the tracker's terse warning. We fell back and let that lady go on. It was too nice a day to get into any arguments with a lioness over rights of way.

Later we came upon one of those dramas which occur in the world of the wild. A sable lay dead under a sausage tree, killed by a lioness. In this ancient battle of tooth, claw, and horns, the lioness, too, had lost. She was immobilized alongside her victim, her back broken.

Reassured that the lioness was indeed incapable of movement by her failure to react to clods and stones thrown at her, we approached cautiously. The lioness watched us quietly, following our movements with great yellow eyes. There was no snarling, no lip curling, no sign of fear or hatred. Pedro took his rifle from the tracker and walked around the lioness. The eyes followed him, unblinking. I decided to study the horizon for a moment as the shot rang out.

We stood there, Pedro and I, looking at each other. John, the tracker, was puzzling over the ground, trying to work out what had happened there. Pedro shrugged, accepted his part in the inevitable.

"She wanted to die," he said. "You could see it in her eyes. She knew what I was going to do and *wanted* me to do it."

"I know. It was in her eyes. It was her time."

"Ah, Bwana understands," John said with obvious approval. He had worked out the puzzle after a close examination of the dead lioness. "She was an old lion and hungry. Otherwise she would never attack a bull sable by herself. She was not strong enough to pull him down and ripped open his neck with her claws and jaws as he threw her into the tree trunk. The tree broke her back, and the sable bled to death." It was that simple: another episode in the endless round of death and life in the bush.

Pedro spoke to John, sending him to bring the pickup. While we waited, seated in the shade of the sausage tree, he asked if I wanted any of the lion's claws or teeth. I declined hastily. That was a very special lion; somehow it would have been sacrilegious to have denuded her in death. Pedro was so patently relieved at my refusal that I must have raised an eyebrow or two. He explained, a bit shamefacedly.

"I want to bury the lion, Jack. She does not deserve to be torn up by vultures." I nodded, understanding, glad that I hadn't become one of the vultures myself. When the pickup arrived, the mechanic and skinner helped us dig a grave, and we buried the lioness under the sausage tree. The sable was gutted and thrown into the pickup for the pot.

There wasn't a whole lot of conversation on the way back to camp, but one odd thing happened. A grysbok jumped from a clump of grass, ran a few feet, stopped, and stared at me. I had never seen one act in such a bold fashion before. The tiny antelopes—about ten pounds— were always quite timid and ran off as fast as they could, dodging and darting like all the devils of hell were after them. Pedro, busy with his driving, did not see it. I was pleased to see it so close, with its sloe–eyes and spindly legs.

On the next day we saw very little game, which surprised us. We stopped for lunch in the shade of some mukuri trees interspersed with thickets of mitundo. About all we had seen were two grey duikers. I assured Pedro that there was no way I was going to shoot a duiker.

"They're too small. I won't shoot any of the pygmy antelopes, unless we're starving."

"You wouldn't *want* one for the pot, even if you *were* starving," Pedro said.

"What's wrong with them?"

"Duikers eat excrement."

"What?"

"Yeah. They eat a lot of it and it taints their meat," Pedro said. "In fact, when we hunt yellow–backed duiker in the rain forest, we get the boys to defecate in the same spot for awhile, to bait them." Pedro's eyes were twinkling.

"Yuk!" I didn't know if he was kidding me or not, but he was enjoying my discomfiture. "In that case I'll just starve, I guess. This is a hell of a conversation to be having with lunch."

"Jack, you're as fussy about your food as a lioness is about who fathers her cubs."

At this point John, who had finished eating, came and sat on his heels.

"What is it, John?"

"It is the Kefundu, Boss. The grysbok." John looked worried.

"What grysbok?"

"The one of yesterday which you did not see. He is wishing to die. He came from the bush and stood, asking us to kill him," John said.

"Oh, shit!" Pedro's reaction astonished me. He turned to me to explain. "The blacks believe that Kefundu, the grysbok, cannot be killed unless he wants to die. They also believe that if you don't kill him when he wants you to, he will scare away all the bigger game until you do shoot him. That's why we saw no game this morning. At least that's what John and the others believe," he ended lamely.

"And obviously you believe it, too," I said.

"We–ell, yes, I guess I do. It's happened to me too many times to be just a superstition. The last time was with a German client. He wouldn't shoot the grysbok which just stood there looking at him. He was after elephant, and there had been plenty of them around. After he refused to shoot that damn little antelope, we couldn't find an elephant of any size or description. Hunted hard for more than a week, saw nothing, I swear to God." Pedro shook his head.

"What happened?"

"We had one hell of a time finding Kefundu again, but we did finally. The German shot him and two days later shot an elephant with 85–pound tusks. That's the God's truth, Jack."

"Okay, I believe you. Strange things happen in this country, no question of that. What do you think we ought to do?"

"If you can remember where you and John saw that antelope, we'd better go looking for him, that's what I think," Pedro said.

"And if we *can't* find him, or he runs off this time?" I asked.

"If he runs off, it is not the one we want. The one we want will be wanting us, and he'll stand there. If we can't find *that* one, I guess we just keep hunting and pray a lot." Pedro smiled, but he wasn't kidding.

Every day, morning and evening, we rode along that road but saw no Kefundu, not even one that ran away. And every day we hunted for eland. Ten days we hunted: to every salt lick in the concession, about two thousand square miles; to the water holes and the river, along every road and crisscross in between; in the pickup and on foot. But we saw no eland—and damned little else. Each day we left camp earlier and hunted harder and longer—five grown men going crazy trying to find a grysbok, net weight ten pounds. All the blacks were depressed, felt hopeless. Next morning we went back over some of the old ground. We saw some kob and hartebeest and a damaliscus, but no eland. At about four we drove into a lovely waterhole, walking the final three–eighths of a mile. With the exception of one lonely warthog, it was completely deserted. Before our encounter with the grysbok, there would have been two dozen animals at that waterhole at four in the afternoon.

Depressed, we were driving back out the track to the main road when John put up a shout. Pedro braked hard. We looked where John was pointing.

Two hundred yards away a male lion lay, head up, staring at us calmly from the top of a big termite mound. With the sinking sun shining on his golden mane, he was a wonderful sight.

Pedro had his glasses on him by the time the rover stopped rolling. The blacks were about to jump out of their shoes from excitement. John tried to hand me a rifle. I was intrigued with the stirring sight but not at all interested in shooting the lion. I don't shoot cats because no one eats them. Pedro knew this; we had hunted together on several safaris.

I thought of the blacks' reaction to the other lions we had seen early in this safari. John and the others had expected me to go after two of the bigger males. The Bembe tribe of which they were members believed the lion to be the greatest of all trophies. Each time John would ask Pedro, "Are we to hunt this leone?" and Pedro would shake his head. Then the three blacks would talk excitedly about the "Bwana, who must be a great lion killer, for he has turned down two mighty fine leones." To their simplistic minds there could be no reason for refusing a lion except that one already had a better one. The thought amused me. I had never shot a lion.

"He is a very old lion," Pedro said.

I nodded. By now I had studied him with my own binocs.

"Won't you please shoot this lion, Jack? He is old and very big."

"No thanks, Pedro."

When John saw me shaking my head again, he spoke up. "Bwana, you will forgive me if I point out that we are trying to hunt under the spell of the Kefundu who was not killed, which means we must fail. Our only chance is to shoot this lion and get the lucky bones from his neck for you. With them we may break the spell and find an eland."

I was touched. Pedro said again, "He is *very* old, Jack. Soon he will become a man–eater if he isn't already. He will be torn apart by wild dogs or hyena. He is too thin to be strong any more."

I nodded. "Give me the gun. I'll go closer and check while I'm thinking about it."

I took the rifle, set the scope up to nine power, and started walking toward the lion. I covered fifty yards, standing straight up in plain sight. He never moved; he could have been a statue. Strange. I sat down, put the scope on him and studied carefully. I could see the vertebrae sticking up along his backbone, could count the ribs on the one side I could partially see. Then I looked at his face. I almost dropped the rifle. The same look! In the eyes, the same look: a quiet and unafraid contemplation of death, exactly what I had seen in the eyes of the lioness with the broken back. He *knew* what I was going to do, as she had known what Pedro would do, and it was all right; it was his time. He knew even before I did.

That night at dinner John came from the village where the celebration of the lion's kill had been going full blast. He shyly held out his huge black hand; in the pinkness of his palm lay two tiny bones, about two inches long, polished white. "The lucky bones, Bwana. Take them tomorrow and we will find eland. Give them to your woman afterward for good luck all your life." I thanked him and placed them in a shirt pocket.

The next day was my last day to hunt. We drove out of camp and headed for the south road, then along it for several miles.

"We'll head across country and just go blind," Pedro told me, "looking for fresh crossing tracks." I nodded.

For about five hours we wandered up and down; over and around logs, stumps, rocks, and trees; through sand, mud and grass eight feet over our heads. I was just becoming aware of a few pangs of hunger when Pedro and John yelled in unison, "Fresh tracks!" They were really fresh; some of the broken twig ends on the bushes were still bleeding sap; at least two bulls, from the tracks.

"Let's go," Pedro said grimly. John started off on the tracks, me right behind. Pedro quickly caught us up, and we hastened after the herd. Two hours later we were still hastening, and I was running out of gas. Once we actually saw the ass–ends of the last two eland just disappearing in the jesse[1], but we couldn't seem to catch them. Pedro finally said, "We'd better rest for a few minutes. They're aware of us anyway; we've got to let them calm down."

We sat, our backs against two maganga trees. It was hot. Our shirts were stuck to our backs with sweat, and the mopane bees—a tiny bee which doesn't sting, about the size of a gnat—were damned near driving me crazy. As I flailed away at them, brushing some off my shirt front, I felt something in my shirt pocket. My hand brought out the two crescent–shaped lucky bones. I had forgotten all about them. I turned them over in my fingers, idly studying them. "Pretty nondescript," I thought and replaced them in the pocket.

"Chasing eland is better than swatting bees. Let's go, Pedro."

We took up the chase again. The animals had made a big swing to the left and were now in some heavy

---

[1]Type of brush.

grass, at least ten feet tall. We were going slow now, trying to make no noise. We could hear them moving slowly ahead; they sounded like a herd of buffalo. By the time the herd reached the edge of the tall grass and began to enter the more open mitombu woodland, we were right on their tails, and I had slid a live round into the rifle barrel. As we broke out of the grass, they were only a hundred yards ahead and running now.

"On the right! The old one on the right!" Pedro was screaming, "Shoot the one on the right!" The sight of over fifty of the huge animals running in "broad front" before me was a bit overwhelming. All I could see were those gigantic hips, the long tail swinging madly back and forth, and the great horns. But I managed to drive a shot through the hip which turned him a bit. The second shot went through the flank, forward into the barrel chest, and the old bull slowed, coming to a full stop underneath a small whistling thorn tree. He stood there, a great grey and brown giant, then slowly sank to the ground.

John pounded my shoulder, laughing and shouting. Pedro literally jumped with his cries of triumph. Finally I made out what John was saying.

"Lucky bones too strong for Kefundu."

THE SALESMAN

His guts hurt and his head ached. The traffic seemed to move in slow motion—God, would they *never* get it in gear? In his frustrated irritation, he was talking to himself, something he did whenever he was angry or tired enough, and tonight he was both.

"C'mon, you miserable bastards. Get out of my way, for Christsake! Jesus, will I be glad to get home." He thought of the drink he was going to make himself when he got there. "Biggest damn glass in the house," he muttered. He rubbed the sides of his jaw with his free hand, feeling the day–end stubble prickle against his finger tips. "Ooo, you crazy son–of–a–bitch, what's the matter with you?" as a car swerved in front of him, requiring the sudden slamming of his brakes. As he gunned it back to keep his place in the traffic, an almost irresistible urge to ram the violator in the rear flowed through his mind, but he thought better of it.

It was imperative that he get home asap, in order to sit

down and relax—unwind. It felt like all his nerves were steel springs, wound so tight as to be near breaking. The thought that he was already sitting down, and could relax as he drove, never crossed his mind. It would not have been part of the ritual—a sacrilege, you might say—for him to relax before he reached home. He would remain wound up tight until he walked through his front door. That was the routine, the way it was done, the way he'd always done it. He had to do it that way—he was a salesman.

Every day he got up, took his turn in the bathroom, dressed, ate a breakfast he only half tasted in the midst of a cacophony of complaining, arguing children's voices, kissed his distracted wife and went out to the car. Every day except some weekends, that is. He got in the car and it all started: the car, the day, the struggle for survival. The day was a battle, and it did not end until he parked the car in the driveway that night, crossed the clipped–lawn moat to the door–gate of his castle, and closed it all behind him outside.

Inside was sanctuary, supposedly. Well, maybe. If the kids were not fighting or crying, if the day had been a good one for his wife. Otherwise he might find he'd traded one battle for another. But at least there was the drink, which made up for a certain amount of strife, especially if it became two, or three.

The city had been left behind now, the congestion was clearing up, and he began to make better time. Once again, his free hand rubbed his jaw–lines, and he suddenly realized that the jaw muscles were sore. What the hell? He rubbed them, puzzled momentarily. Maybe lockjaw, he thought, and grinned at the nonsense of the thought. The movement of the muscles to make the grin was enough to resolve the puzzle for him. The day had involved an unusual number of interviews, and he had smiled so much that his jaws were sore. "Jesus," he thought. "I've got salesman's cheeks." This made him smile even more, and the pain increased a bit. "Damn!" He clamped his mouth closed and frowned. "That actually hurts."

His street at last, and gratefully he turned into the driveway. Inside, he greeted the kids and his wife, took off his necktie and opened the collar of his shirt with a sigh of relief. Pausing as he turned from hanging his coat in the closet, he stood before the mirror, looking at his face thoughtfully. He scowled at himself, twisting his face into several grimaces. It felt good—stretched the sore muscles. His wife came in, watched in surprise a moment, and asked,

"What in the world do you think you're doing?"

"I smiled so much today that my face is sore. I'm making up for it, evening it up. Anyway, it relaxes the muscles."

"Well, stop it. You'll scare the kids, and it gives me the creeps watching you make those horrible faces."

"Okay." He wandered into the kitchen, made both of them a drink. They sat down and chatted perfunctorily about their "days." The conversation was mindless, almost automatic. His mind was not on it. He was thinking about the smiling.

He thought about the people, the ones he had done all the smiling for. Prospects—prospective sales—nothing more. They were not friends, never would be, and really meant nothing to him beyond the possibility of a sale. Some of them he had even disliked, but they had received the same quota of smiles—"sincere" smiles—as the ones he liked.

He found the concept a bit sickening, it made him feel sort of dirty somehow. Not that he had said anything unethical or untrue to make a sale—this he would never do. He prided himself on selling only what was needed and could be afforded, nothing more. But he also prided himself on his honesty, and the smiles—at least some of them—smacked almost of dishonesty. Was it honest to pretend friendliness to someone you really didn't like?

He suffered these self–doubts often, for he hated being a salesman. He really hated it. Asking someone to buy, risking the horror of horrors, a refusal, was more than difficult, it was painful. Having hypothetical doors slammed in his face constantly was enough to shrivel his soul. He'd wanted to be an educator, but working his way through college during the thirties had been difficult enough, graduate school was out of the question. He'd gone to work at whatever he could find, and in 1937 that wasn't much.

It was one of those quirks of fate that keep the devil chortling which had prescribed his ending up a salesman. Two facts kept him at it: one was that he was good—he could make more money selling than any other way—and the second was that four kids and a wife needed a fair amount of food and other knick–knacks. He worked in a pressure cooker of his own making—strictly on commission, no salary. He was responsible only to himself, if he made sales he made money; if he didn't, it was his tough luck. His and his family's.

This meant that the salesman must be more than just good at selling, because he must do everything for himself. Tell himself when to go to work, how long to work, plan his time efficiently, find his own prospects, manage his finances, keep up with changing laws and taxes—he was employee, employer, manager, controller, research department, file clerk, secretary, all rolled into one.

There was no one else, if he needed help or advice. No one to give him encouragement, praise, or counsel. In the mornings it was his job to say, "Get up, get going." In the evenings, his job to plan the next day. In between, his job to keep saying "You can do it," or often "Forget it, you did your best. Go on to the next one. The law of averages is with you."

The salesman drove himself. He worked against quotas, set by himself—weekly quotas, annual quotas. It left precious little time for self–congratulation or relaxation after a good week or a good year. No matter how successful *this* week was, next week was only two days away, and it had to be done all over again. Double his quota this week did not let him off the hook for the next week's quotas.

The salesman worked nights when necessary. He worked anytime, every time—whenever he could get someone to listen. Weekends, Saturday nights, all kinds of hours. And he managed to make the quotas—they were the whip with which he drove himself—they would only work as long as he succeeded in filling them, he knew.

It was not only the smiling that bothered him about selling. There were two other things that were even worse. One was the waiting, the time that comes in every sale when the sales talk is finished and he had to sit, silent, waiting for the "yes." This was the crucial time, when one word too many could destroy the sale. It had taken years for him to learn to recognize that moment when it came, and he could never handle it without becoming very tense inside—though of course he made sure that his outward appearance belied the tension, as it must for the sale to be successful.

There had been times when he had to sit, apparently relaxed, and smiling, for as long as four or five minutes; watching the prospects sweat as they cast about for some objection which could be raised. It was the moment of truth, a test of will power and self control. Most often he won, but it extracted an awful price. Many times the adrenaline flowed for several hours afterward, and he was too stimulated to fall asleep when he got home, though exhausted mentally and physically.

The other thing that bothered him was the worst part of selling—it was the turndown, the "no." It almost destroyed him when it happened, and the thinking about it, the fearing of it was almost intolerable. It implied so much more than just a failure, though for him, that was bad enough. To be told "no" carried implications of lack of approval, dislike, and attacked the very foundations of his own feeling of self–worth.

Then, just as his ego was lying around him in ripped shreds, he must force himself to try again, to risk the horrible experience all over. No time allowed for wound–licking or souls rebuilding for the salesman. He held in his guts a full knowledge of the pathos and heartbreak that lie behind the words of that old chestnut, "a salesman travels on nothing more than a shoeshine and a smile."

The voice of his wife broke into his reverie, he heard a new note of concern in it. "The dentist says that we should take Susan to an orthodontist. There is something wrong with her bite. He gave me the name of one he said was good."

"Better do it, then," the salesman replied, doing his best to keep any note of resignation out of his own voice. "Get an estimate from him on the costs, and how fast he wants to be paid."

"Can we afford it? The dentist said it usually costs two thousand, more or less."

"Whew! That much? Don't worry, we'll afford it okay," the salesman replied, making a mental note to push the quotas one notch higher. "Let's eat, I think I'm unwound now."

"Are you going out afterward?"

"Not tonight. I couldn't line up an interview." As she began to serve the meal, he realized that she had fed the children early so they could eat in peace. He was grateful for that. His thoughts returned to the smiling. He wondered if he would ever have enough money to be able to smile only when he felt like it. To be able to not really care if he made a sale or not. To not have to work with anyone he disliked, to not have to sweat out the yes or no of any prospect. That would indeed be heaven, he thought—but it would mean he was no longer a salesman. He would have become an order–taker. A few more years could do it, if he could keep up the pace. He could hardly wait, it couldn't happen to a nicer guy. The salesman's wife wondered at his quiet smile—it didn't seem to bother his sore cheeks.

AFRICANER

Rowan knocked the dottle from his pipe and put it in his pocket. He looked at the horse again, then back to the Africaner and shook his head.

"He's definitely no better, Jon. Maybe worse. What do you think?"

The Africaner shifted his huge bulk and rose slowly to his feet. He took off the great floppy hat and scratched his shaggy head, then replaced it.

"He's plenty sick, that horse. You still think it's colic?"

"I'm no vet, Jon, but I think that's what it is. Maybe some more medicine? There's half a bottle left."

"Let's give him the lot—kill him or cure him, maybe."

The Africaner spoke even more slowly than usual, obviously troubled. Rowan nodded, got the bottle, and together they tried to force the horse's mouth open. It was a big horse, big enough to carry a man the size of the Africaner all day long. Not every horse could do that. The horse fought them, slipped and fell heavily on its side in the straw. He struggled to get back up, his legs thrashing the air and scattering the straw in all directions. Fearful that his struggles might result in a broken leg, the two men tried to hold him down, to calm him, but the horse was beyond control.

The battle between the men and the horse took on epic proportions. In the cramped quarters of the stall, medicine forgotten, the men struggled to hold the horse's head and front quarters down, at the same time twisting and jumping to avoid the slashing steel–shod hooves. The horse screamed and flailed, kicked out at man and wood and air. The men held fast. Neither felt he could quit; to leave the other exposed alone invited serious injury. Neither spoke; grunts, gasps, pantings, thumps, and bangs served to unify their efforts. The snorts and screams from the horse, the sounds from the men, filled the barn with noise.

Minutes passed. Struggling to secure the horse's rearing head, Rowan felt his strength going fast. He had never seen a horse act this way; it seemed to have gone completely mad. The Africaner, fighting to immobilize the front quarters by himself, a gleam in his eyes of raw pleasure, seemed as strong as ever. He is actually enjoying the battle, Rowan thought. His own energy was rapidly dissipating, and he was getting a bit desperate. Suddenly the horse gave up the struggle. It lay quietly, nostrils flared out and rib cage heaving as it fought for air. Weak–kneed, Rowan moved to the wall and slumped down in the straw. Jon sat on his haunches by the horse, patting it on the neck and crooning softly to it.

Rested, Rowan finally said:

"I don't think it's colic, Jon. That horse was clear out of its head. Has it been injured recently?"

"Nothing important. Some scratches from a wire about two weeks ago, but they healed up, no problem."

"Ah, maybe that's it. He acted like he had tetanus. If so, he's in the final throes. We're not going to save him."

"Yes, I think he dies now," Jon said. "Well, he was a good horse. He gave us a good fight." A smile broke out on the Africaner's face at the memory. "You are sure of it, Rowan?"

"I'm afraid so. The wild animals act crazy like that when they have tetanus. But I'm no vet."

"You are the next best thing—a Parks Department zoologist. It's lucky you came to my ranch for visit yesterday when I needed help."

The Africaner went for the rifle, got in his pickup, and backed it into the barn as Rowan waited. He got out, slid a round into the barrel of the gun and snapped home the bolt. The shot filled the small barn once again with noise.

On his way to visit Jon at the ranch again, Rowan

chuckled as he recalled the circumstances which had resulted in his meeting the Africaner. Before coming to farm in Rhodesia, Jon had been the chief of an anti–poaching unit in Kruger Park. The two hundred and seventy pound Africaner hated poachers with a passion, and some of his methods were unique, though extremely effective. Poachers who were caught were handcuffed—a usual procedure—to a tree and left there, a procedure *not* so usual. Jon and his men would return in two weeks to retrieve the handcuffs, by that time licked clean.

On one occasion two poachers had shot some elephants. Jon went after them with two game scouts. They caught one poacher and killed him before he could get out of the Park; the other escaped into Mozambique. Jon sent his scouts back with the dead poacher and followed the escaped one across the border. Finally catching him up, he killed him. The fellow was large, perhaps two–hundred pounds, and the thought of carrying his body all the way back to Park headquarters struck Jon as just a bit impractical. He needed the body as evidence, however. The solution? Jon cut the body in half and took the upper slice back to headquarters. His supervisors found this a bit too much, and the Africaner found himself among the unemployed. Hence to Rhodesia and the farm.

When Rowan arrived, there was no one about the house or the corrals. His yells brought no response, and he was on the point of leaving when he heard the sound of a vehicle approaching from the direction of the big pasture. In moments Jon's pickup drove up to the corrals, and the Africaner got out to greet him.

"Hallo, Rowan. How do things go at the station?" He did not wait for an answer. "It is good to see you, my friend. Come look what I've got in the back here." He pointed to the pickup's box back and started toward it with Rowan following. He proudly displayed his cargo: two lions, a male and a female, lying quite dead—or so it appeared. As he explained to his friend that the lions had been "bothering cattle," a low growl emanated from the pickup, followed by the male suddenly coming to life before their eyes and staggering over the side to the ground. A bit wobbly, he was heading for somewhere else, which was exactly what Rowan had in mind for himself.

The two friends parted company in a hurry. The Africaner headed for the lion. When Rowan looked back, the Africaner had the lion by the tail with one hand and was holding a five–foot crowbar in the other.

"Rowan," he yelled, "won't you help me load my lion? He is a bit heavy for me." The grin on his face was from ear to ear.

"Not until he's a lot quieter than he is right now," Rowan replied. "You can sort this one out by yourself."

"Okay, my friend. As you wish." Jon gave a prodigious jerk on the tail of the snarling lion, swung the "quieter," and hit the big cat right between the ears. There was a sickening crunch, and the cat went limp. "Come now. Give me a hand here, and we'll take them to the skinning tent."

After off–loading the lions at the tent—having made sure they were both really dead this time—Jon announced, "You must come see my new horse. He's a dandy."

He led the way back to the barn and through it. In back, in a small pasture, was the biggest, blackest horse Rowan had ever seen that wasn't hitched to a fire engine.

"He's a real beauty," Rowan marveled. "God, he's big. Must be seventeen hands, Jon."

"Just over," Jon said proudly. "He's one–half Clydesdale. But he is fast, too. He is no truck horse. I will show you."

He picked up a rope halter off the fence, opened the gate, and walked toward the horse, saying, "hoo, hoo, hoo" softly. The big stallion eyed the man suspiciously, nickered a bit, tossed his head several times, and trotted away to the other corner of the pasture. Still crooning, Jon turned toward him and walked slowly forward. Rowan viewed the scene with enjoyment: the huge man with his great flopping hat, the dark shiny coat of the equally huge horse, the green of the pasture against the colorful background of the bush.

Jon's patience prevailed over his horse's suspicions,

and they returned to the gate where Jon tied the halter rope to a fence rail. After a brief trip to the barn, the Africaner reappeared, his arms filled with saddle, bridle, two blankets, and a martingale. Rowan's eyebrows shot up a trifle as he noticed the latter, but he made no comments.

The horse stood quietly for the saddling, only the constant twitching of the muscles along his flanks indicating any nervousness. There was a look in his eyes, however. Rowan studied the horse, then the man. There was a look in *his* eye, too. Each of them had been there before, Rowan decided, and each knew what was coming—was looking forward to it, in fact, with some relish.

"Is your horse fully broken, Jon?" he asked innocently.

"As gentle as the lamb of Mary." The grin on his face was disarming and open. "You would like to ride him, Rowan?"

Rowan had to admire the straight face with which his friend asked the question. "Thanks, old friend, but I think I'll just watch for a bit."

"Goot. I take out the kinks for you. Then you try, maybe."

He finished checking the fit of the cinch, martingale, and bridle, took the reins in one hand, untied the rope and coiled it against the saddle. Then he led the horse back and forth for a few minutes. He pulled the big floppy hat lower on his head, turned a stirrup backwards, and slid his foot into it. One quick, supple movement and he was in the saddle. Momentarily.

The horse's head went down between his forelegs; his back arched and headed skyward; the hindquarters headed east, the front west. He came down stiff–legged, jarring the Africaner hard. Jon let out a bellow of delight, a primeval roar of sheer animal joy that rose from deep in his guts. Dust boiled up around them, the horse swapping ends and spinning in a blur of violent motion. Above it all, the great hat flopped madly up and down.

Despite the restraining martingale, the horse rose up on his hind legs, front legs pawing the air until it appeared he would fall over backwards. But he came down and took off in a series of stiff–legged jumps— sidewinding, sun–fishing, and twisting his heaving withers and hips across the corral. There were times when he was looking south as his tail went past him headed north.

This was no temporary fit of nervous energy being worked off, Rowan realized. It was a testing, a battle for supremacy between two magnificent animals, each accustomed to absolute rule. It had been fought out before, and the horse had won often enough to remain optimistic about the outcome; that was apparent. But he was not going to win this one; that, too, was apparent. The jumps became shorter, the twisting less violent.

Finally, the horse stopped bucking, and leveled out into a full run along the corral fence. Jon yelled something to Rowan and pointed to the outer gate. Rowan managed to get there and fling it open one jump ahead of them, which saved the gate for further use. Nothing made of wood could have stopped that horse.

Stretched out in a level run, the truth of Jon's earlier claim was substantiated: the horse was fast. The long legs covered yards of turf at every stride, and the black stallion and its rider began to disappear in the distance. For a time Rowan could still see the Africaner's big feet bouncing in the stirrups, the big hat flopping about his ears.

In moments they were back, coming at a dead run and sliding to a dusty, rock–spattering stop in front of Rowan. He stood shaking his head and looked up at Jon's grinning, sweaty face.

"That's some horse, my friend. I'd hardly say he was fully broken, though."

"Ah, you worry about nothing, Rowan. He is gentle as a baby lamb. A little playful, maybe."

"Playful! You old rogue. I'll wait till next year to ride him, when he's a bit less playful. Does he answer the rein, can you spin him around?"

"Ha! You do not know the horse I cannot turn around."

The Africaner's swollen biceps contracted on the reins. The horse's head came up; the martingale tightened; the front feet came off the ground. Jon's left hand jerked off his hat and slapped the horse's head with it while his right hand continued to lift and pull the reins to the right. The horse staggered on its hind legs and spun, ending up on all four feet headed in the opposite direction.

"You see? He turns fine, doesn't he?"

"Do you turn him that way all the time?" Rowan was astonished. "You have to stop him if you want to turn him?"

"Yes, but he goes like hell when I get him headed in the right direction."

BOOTIE

The relationship between a professional hunter and his client is at best unpredictable. At worst—forget the whole thing. It begins like a sparring match, two strange dogs sniffing each other out in cautious and casual—on the surface—circlings. After all, each is entrusting his very life to the other, in more ways than one.

There are the obvious ways, of course: a complete stranger with a high–powered rifle alongside, or, even worse, behind you in wild and dangerous terrain, crowding dangerous and/or wounded animals. These are par for the course, to be expected. But there are other ways, some of them quite unexpected. Bootie was a case in point.

He picked me up at the Lasaka airport about three–thirty in the afternoon. A tallish, good–looking young fellow with the ubiquitous Toyota pickup. We piled all my katunda in the back and drove out onto the highway leading north toward Bangwelu Swamp and the safari camp.

"I understand that you're most interested in a Sitatunga?" he inquired as we moved up to what apparently was his usual cruising speed in the Toyota.

"Right," I replied as I noted a complete lack of movement from the arrow on the speedometer. "What's wrong with your odometer?"

"Oh, nothing, really. I just disconnected it," he said.

For a moment silence reigned inside the pickup. "Disconnected it?" I chewed that one over in my mind.

"Yeah, it was causing too much nervousness in my clients."

"Oh *boy*," I thought. "Here we go again." Two months before I'd been through all kinds of hell with another P. Hunter from this same safari company, including a twenty–five minute ride in a chartered plane with the needle on empty on the fuel gauge. You are entitled to ask at this point what I was doing back there with the same company. It was the damned Sitatunga.

If one wants to shoot a Sitatunga, one must go where there *are* some of these elusive swamp antelope, and that means Banguelu Swamp, or Okavangu Swamp. Banguelu was far and away the best bet of the two, and it was the exclusive concession of Bootie's boss. So, here I was again. I thought of my previous misfortune:

"Is that idiot McKay still hunting with you guys?" I asked.

"Nah, he brought a group of Italians in to hunt birds

down at Kafue, in spite of being told that there *were* no birds at Kafue. After three days they all came back to headquarters in Lusaka and wandered around shooting all the dicky birds they could find for two days. Then the boss kicked out the lot of them and sent McKay packing." Bootie was quiet for a moment while he negotiated a turn and several chuck holes in the high-way at whatever speed the odometer wasn't recording, then continued, "That guy was *really* crazy."

"Tell me about it," I muttered. "Not to mention half blind, paranoid and cruel. I spent the most miserable two weeks of my life with him."

"Well, maybe we can make up for it this trip." The conversation turned to more pleasant things.

"How long will it take us to reach camp? Last time we flew." The thought occurred to me that we were doing a reasonably accurate facsimile in the Toyota, but I didn't mention it. I didn't want to make *him* nervous; too many chuck holes in that "highway."

"About five or six hours, if we don't have any problems," Bootie replied. At which point there was a solid "clunk" from underneath us, and one wheel began to chatter as he brought the pickup to a stop at the roadside.

Bailing out, we found the problem; one tire had lost a chunk of casing about the size of a small plate. The tube, luckily, was still intact. Moving the katunda, we retrieved the spare, and soon we were back on the road, dodging chuck holes at "cruising" speed — whatever that was. Whatever it was, it was plenty.

By this time we were about one hundred and twenty miles north of Lusaka, traveling through an area of singular uninhabitation. There weren't even isolated huts and shambas along the roadside any longer. The sun was flirting with the horizon, the day had about run its course. Some shut-eye struck me as a good idea after the long plane ride to Lusaka. Famous last ideas, you might say.

A horrendous explosion put an end to any thoughts of shut-eye in a hurry. The pickup careened toward the right shoulder of the highway at enormous speed, listing badly, all tires screaming in protest. For one long, terrifying moment we were almost on our side, then whiplashing wickedly, we began rolling from side to side, sliding and skidding. Slowly the momentum diminished until Bootie could bring us to a welcome halt. All in one piece, all upright.

"Whew, that was one super driving job!" I said to Bootie, and I really meant it. We must have been doing over seventy when the blowout occurred, and an overloaded Toyota pickup is one top heavy, unguided missile.

"Son of a bitch!" was the angry reply.

"Good Lord! I'm just delighted to still be alive. What are you so mad about? Count your blessings," I advised him.

"I am," he said. "We're a hundred and twenty-five miles from the nearest town, where we just *might* find a tire to fit this beast if we're *very* lucky. We no longer have a spare. There's very little traffic on this road in the daytime, which is going fast, and none at night. We are forty miles from the turn-off to camp, which is forty more miles to camp in the other direction.

"Let's see now. Have I forgotten anything? Oh yes, we do have some food and water."

"And we're alive and unharmed," I added softly. Bootie was silent. I suppose it never occurred to him that we might have died. It's great to be young.

I began to think about our predicament more carefully. "How far to turn off the highway?"

"Forty miles or so."

"And then to camp?"

"Another forty. On a damn rough dirt and rock road," he added.

"Well!" We walked to the roadside and sat on some rocks. After some moments I said, "We've still got the first tire with the bad casing. The hole is on the side. I think it will hold up as long as it doesn't get too hot or hit a rock. We can take it plenty slow and head back to town. It's worth a try. If it blows, we start walking."

Bootie perked right up. "You know, that just might work, at that," he said. "But I'm damned if I want to head back to town. How fast do you think it would be safe to go on that cripple?"

"Fifteen miles an hour," I replied. "*Maybe* twenty on smooth spots. We can try it for a few miles at ten, check the tire—feel for heat—and should be able to tell how fast that way." I'd forgotten the non-working odometer.

"Okay. Let's change the thing and get going. Toward camp."

"Camp? We'll just make things worse if it doesn't work. The tire probably won't take the rough road."

"And we'll have our hunt if it does. There's one thing I never told you. A black farmer lives in a house at the turn-off. I think he just might have a tire that will fit this truck. If he does, it will solve the rough road for us. And there's a trailer in camp that has the same size tires, for *sure*."

"If we ever get there" crossed my mind. The whole thing was a bit out of my area, however, and I decided to let Bootie make the decisions. We got the damaged tire out, replaced it on the pickup, and once more started up the highway. Dusk had arrived by then, with the sudden blackness of the African night right on its heels. The contrast in our speed was immense. Everything had gone into slow motion as we seemed to be fixed in walls of blackness.

The odometer useless, Bootie had to drive by "feel;" we had no idea what our actual speed might be. When the tire made a noise, we slowed until the noise stopped.

"You really think this farmer might have a tire that will fit us, and that he would part with it?" I asked. The thought was boggling my mind. We were really out in the middle of nowhere. Black farmers were scarce in this area of rock and swamp, to say the least; the Toyota used a tire that fit only Toyotas; black farmers are lucky to have an ox, let alone a vehicle. "What do we do if he doesn't?"

"We worry about that when it happens," Bootie replied. I decided to get a head start.

Eventually a light appeared in the darkness ahead. It was almost eleven o'clock. "Turn off?" I asked.

"Yep, hope he's still up," Bootie replied. The source of the light was a white gas lantern. I wondered what the hell the guy could be doing to keep him up this late; he sure wasn't watching T.V. We chugged slowly into the yard, and Bootie got out to look for the farmer. I looked about the place.

A barn, or large shed on one side, the house on the other. Meager items of tools and equipment parked helter-skelter. A large Acacia tree behind with a tire dangling from a rope for a child's swing. Whatever hope I had mustered was ebbing fast.

A large black man appeared from the house and joined Bootie. I could see them gesturing as they talked. They moved over to the swing and examined the tire. What the hell? The farmer untied the rope. Bootie examined the tire more carefully, and bounced it on the ground several times. I couldn't believe my eyes. He shook hands with the farmer and brought the tire over to the Toyota. I could see where the tire's casing had been squeezed together by the rope. It looked old and sort of brittle.

"Well, I was right," Bootie grinned at me. "It will fit, and it's still in one piece, which is more than I can say for our own. It will get us to camp."

And it did, about three o'clock in the morning. Don't think I was ever so glad to see camp. But a swing? To deliberately drive *away* from town into the bush on the forlorn hope that a child's swing might fit? Oh, well. It's just Africa.

THE BOY

He sat, straddling the wooden board fence, dreaming in the afternoon sun. He was happy to be there, alone with his thoughts. Somehow the height of the fence had presented him with both a challenge and a sanctuary, and he had puzzled over the ascent for some moments before taking advantage of the young apple tree growing close along side, shinnying up the slick trunk to clamber along a spreading branch and pass, teetering precariously, to the fence top. His goal achieved, he could rest complacently—at peace—undisturbed.

His two younger brothers and mother were napping inside the house. It was a good feeling, free of control and supervision, free from competition and intrusion on his space. His wooden steed was solid and firm between his legs, the border of his kingdom limited only by the strength of his imagination. Since he had only yesterday celebrated his ninth birthday, that was almost without limit. His content was complete, untroubled.

The quiet, almost unnoticed, hum of insects was the only sound, slowly hypnotizing him, carrying him off to his own world as he stared, eyes open but unseeing, at the narrow dirt road and path that ran before the house, ten feet in front of his perch.

The spell, the sunny warm peace, was suddenly broken as a sharp, strident voice intruded into his world, dragging him reluctantly back to reality.

"Well, are you going to answer me or not?" The tone was irritable, impatient, reminiscent of some strict school teachers he had known. As he sat in puzzled awakening, unable to answer because he had heard no question, mute with embarrassment, the voice continued, "It's easy to see you have not had a proper bringing–up, young man. Weren't you taught to speak when spoken to? I'll ask you again. Does this path lead to the viewpoint?"

The boy, peering through the platinum blond hair which had fallen over his eyes, made out his questioner on the path before him. An old lady—to his nine year old eyes—in a long brown coat with a fur collar, tapping her walking stick impatiently. The look on her face was grim, angry, tight–lipped. He managed a feeble "Yes," and watched as she turned to walk up the path, straight–backed, unbending. He heard her say as she passed from earshot, "What a rude boy!"

"Take the right–hand fork in the trail," he shouted.

She continued down the path toward the trail but gave no sign that she had heard him. A feeling of deep embarrassment enveloped him; he was ashamed and, at the same time, felt helpless. The peace and contentment of his reverie destroyed, he wondered about the woman. Who was she? She was a stranger to the village, of that he was sure—but where was she going? Up the trail to the viewpoint? It was six miles, uphill most of the way—he had walked it one day with his father—and it was very poorly marked. He wondered as he considered her age, her aloneness, the hours of daylight left. He knew it would be foggy, cold and windy as soon as she was half–way up the ridge.

Mostly, he thought of her anger and her dislike of him, and the memory made him uncomfortable. This was the first time he had faced reprimand and disapproval from a complete stranger. He found it different from that which he had experienced before—from family members, peer groups, school authorities. He could not understand why it was different, but it was. He wondered, what can you do about someone who dislikes you without even knowing you? He decided that it didn't make any sense to dislike her in return, though he certainly hadn't liked what she said.

He was still sitting on the fence when his mother called. The naps were over and he should now take his younger brothers to the small creek flowing behind the house, to keep an eye on them while they picked enough blackberries for tonight's dinner. The matter of the lady passed from his mind.

After breakfast the next day, the boy and his brothers took their daily walk through the lanes of the village to the post office. This was always a treat, for they passed the bakery shop on the way. A Danish lady and her daughter ran the tiny bakery which had display cases in the front room of their home. The boy was fascinated by the delicious smells and spent considerable time admiring everything before they purchased their daily ration of shortbread cookies.

At the post office, he noted an atmosphere of controlled excitement among the adults gathered there, and he contrived to wander from one group to another, eavesdropping on conversations in an effort to discover the cause. As he listened the story began to unfold.

Someone was missing. Since yesterday afternoon. No one had an idea where to start looking for the missing person. The last time anyone had seen her was about three o'clock yesterday afternoon. Her? A premonition sent a chill through him. Could it be his old lady? He tried to get someone's attention, with no success. Everyone was far too busy making plans for a rescue effort to listen to a nine year old boy. He felt frustrated and almost desperate, knowing that if this really was his lady (that was the way he was beginning to think of her), he, then, would have been the last person to see her, and he knew where they should start looking.

Finally, he approached the general delivery window, realizing that someone would have to listen to him there.

The postmistress smiled at him, gave his mail and turned back to her conversation with the sheriff's deputies. The boy almost shouted at her in his haste, "Wait, please," and when he had her attention again, he asked, "Did she have a brown coat with a fur collar?"

"For goodness sake, boy! How do I know if she...?" An odd look came over her face as she studied the boy. Turning to the deputies she said, "Come here a minute, John," One of the men walked to the window and she spoke to him in tones too low for the boy to hear. The man turned to him.

"How do you know she had a brown coat with a fur collar, son?"

"I saw a lady with a coat like that yesterday."

"Do you remember when it was? What time of day?"

"Yes, I do. It was about four o'clock."

"Where was this, that you saw her? And did she say anything to you?"

"Yes." The boy blushed at the memory but continued, "She was on the street in front of my house, the street that ends at the start of the trail to the viewpoint. She wanted to know if the path led to the trail. I told her it did."

"Which way did she go, did you notice?"

"She went down the path toward the trail."

"You're sure about all this, son? It's mighty important."

"Yes, I'm sure." The boy watched as the men gathered in a group and the man called John talked rapidly to the others. Then four of the men got in a car and headed down the road that went along the coast, around the point and back up the other side of the peninsula. The road dead–ended at the viewpoint, the boy knew, but it was trip of nearly forty miles. Several others headed for their horses, mounted and rode up the lane that led to the street where the trail began. No one paid any more attention to the boy, so he called his brothers and they walked slowly home to give his mother the mail. He said nothing to his brothers. They were only five and three and would not understand.

He spent the rest of the day watching the path to the trail—even taking his lunch out to the front porch—he was worried about the old lady and hoped that someone would find her. He thought of the bleak, foggy mountain, and its cold. He hoped the lady wasn't lost there. He remembered what had happened two summers ago. The details came rushing back to him.

He was on a blanket, at the edge of a stream. He couldn't sleep; he wasn't the least bit sleepy. The pleasant murmuring of the small mountain stream that tumbled over the rocks on its irresistible way to the valley had lulled his mother and two younger brothers, but to him its message was an invitation. His father had left them after lunch to go fishing upstream, and he decided to follow and find him. He sat up, saw the others were asleep on the blanket, and quietly started out, following a faint trail which bordered the stream.

It was his first experience with camping, but in another month he would be seven years old, and it never occurred to him that his father might not easily be found. The rocks and bushes along the stream side, the logs and windfalls were large obstacles to his six–year–old body, causing him to struggle where an adult might walk easily—it was slow going, but he persevered obstinately. When he looked back, the camp was out of sight, but he felt no qualms. Surely his father would not be much further ahead now.

The path, such as it was, had long since petered out into the undisturbed jumble of driftwood, logs, bedraggled bushes and all manner and size of granite boulders which winter storms leave scattered along the banks of a mountain trout stream. Some of this debris was of gigantic proportions to the boy and required lengthy detouring. A few of the detours were extensive enough to take him beyond eyesight of the stream. It was only a matter of time until he made a wrong turn, heading away from it altogether. Not long after that, he realized that he had lost the stream. As he continued, more and more desperate to find again his only link to father and family, the horrible truth became obvious at last. He was lost.

Which way should he go? Eyes can see little when they are only three feet from the ground. They see even less when they are full of tears.

He called out, tentatively at first, then louder; finally, at the top of his childish falsetto. The weeping "Daddies" were quite futile, of course, but he was unaware of that. The stream's noise would drown out any other sound. His father might as well be on the moon. The boy kept moving, searching. As his fears grew he forgot all caution, and tried to hurry, running and calling.

He promptly fell headlong. He scrambled up without hesitation to continue his search, driven by desperation. Another fall, and another. He was beyond thinking now, frantic. It was not long before he fell heavily, knocking the breath from his lungs momentarily. The pain reached through the haze of his panic, and he lay there gasping for air, trying to shake off the hurt for several moments. Shaken, he finally recovered and began to run again. It was as if being lost was a thing, something he was trying to get away from, and he had to run to escape it.

He had listened, hoping for some answer to his desperate calls, but heard only the wind through the pine tops. He was tiring now, and stumbled with fatigue. Only the fear kept him going. Falling again, he could not get to his feet this time. His voice was worn down to a mere croak, and he gave up calling. As he sat there on the gravelly bank of a small ridge, the panic and fear grew into hysteria, and he heard voices. They seemed to be coming from the other side of the ridge. He turned and started to claw his way up to the top on his hands and knees.

The stones in the dirt tore the ends of his fingers until the blood began to flow, but he scrambled on, spurred by frantic hope. All the way to the top he heard voices—murmuring, the words indistinguishable—and his head poked over the ridge expecting to see people. Tear–streaked, scratched, his face turned this way and that in a futile search—there was nothing, only trees and more trees. The voices were, he realized now, only in his head. He sank back, sobbing, sliding down the ridge on knees and hands without caring. Exhausted, physically and emotionally, he gave up—he would die here and no one would ever find him, he would never see his mother or father again.

He sat there in total despair. Finally, without any real purpose, he rose to his feet and started walking aimlessly, hardly noticing—or caring—where he was going. He walked simply because there was nothing else for him to do. Until he found an obstacle barring his way. A small gully, perhaps five feet deep, as much across. At the bottom of the gully there was a small amount of water. He looked for an easy way to cross, beginning to think now, all the struggle gone out of him.

Water? His mind began to turn this over, even as he suddenly realized he was terribly thirsty, and slid down into the gully for a drink. His thirst slackened, he stood beside the water, watching the small trickle meander slowly through the gully. Where was it going? Down hill, of course. Where would it end? He thought about it, his six–year–old brain slowly formulating a plan.

The trickle knew where it was going—it would eventually reach a stream. He would follow it, perhaps the stream would be the same one he had lost. The thought gave him renewed hope, renewed strength. He started down the gully. It was hard going in the gully–bottom, he looked with longing at the level bank top, it would be so much easier there. No, he decided—that was how he'd gotten lost in the first place—he stuck to the bottom, even walking right in the water. The water was his security, his only link back to people and life. He was not going to leave it for any reason.

His shoes were soaked, his pants torn and wet; his hands and fingers had stopped bleeding, and he had stopped crying now. He was tired, and sometimes lost his balance and fell because of it. But he kept on dog-gedly, determined to make it no matter how far. His face was streaked with dirt, his hair a tangled mat of needles mixed with the red mountain soil.

Gradually the gully widened, the trickle became a tiny creek, and eventually he arrived at the outlet, where it joined the large stream. He stared at it questioning.

Was it *his* stream? It looked similar, but he recognized nothing. How could he be sure? Bewildered, he began to feel the stirring of his old panic again. Grimly, he fought it off—that was the way to disaster. He must *think* his way out of this. What was he to do? Was it his stream or not, and if it was, should he go up or downstream? That was his enigma.

The decision was simple when he thought of it. He would assume that it was his stream—because if it wasn't, there was nothing he could do about it, he wouldn't know where to look for it and anyway, he was too tired and the sun was no longer high—and he would go downstream, because it was easier, and the way to people would be that way, no matter what stream it might be. He started off.

His progress was slower now, he had to rest often. Sometimes when he rested he reconsidered his decision, but always it seemed the best one to him, so he kept on. The boy reached a point where the stream seemed familiar—could he dare hope?—but he was not sure. He kept on, struggling over and around the boulders. His mind was tired now, as tired as his body, and he was moving in a state of trance, automatic, unthinking. He fought his way up over a bar of gravel at a turning of the stream, and his weary heart leaped with relief and joy. He could see the camp, his mother watching the two brothers playing in the sand at the stream–edge.

The feelings that washed through him were so

violent that the emotions left him weak–kneed and shaky–legged. He could scarcely walk the last one hundred yards. Then his mother saw him and came running. He was safe in her arms, and terribly, terribly tired. The scratches on his face left no scars, but the experience had left some on his memory. The boy shivered as he lived again, in memory, the terror of the experience. He hoped the lady wasn't lost.

That night his father came to spend the weekend with them, and the boy told him everything except what the lady had said. He was ashamed of that.

The next morning his father went to the post office to learn if anyone had found her. No one had. The boy was feeling worse now. Perhaps, he thought, I could have said something to stop her. He asked his father if they could go up the trail and try to find her. After lunch they walked all the way to the viewpoint, looking for tracks and the lady. But they found nothing. That night he was very tired and had bad dreams.

His father checked again the following day but there had been no sign of her. She had vanished. But his father did learn that the lady had been unhappy, and that people were speculating that she had gone up the trail to end her life. He discussed this possibility with the boy. That afternoon he left to return to the city and his work.

The boy climbed to his perch on the fence several times after that, to sit in the warm sun and think about the lady. There were many unanswered questions in his mind. He decided that it would have made no difference if he had spoken to her about the trail, and that made him feel better.

She was not found during the remaining time, before they went home to the city, and they never returned to the village for another summer vacation. In a few years he had to stop being a boy, but he never stopped wondering about the lady.

MEG

The dust devil swirled its unsteady way past the door of the tin shack, and Meg sighed with resignation as a backeddy deposited a coating of fine red dust over everything It is so impossible to keep this place clean, she thought, as she picked up the broom once more. Clem, her husband, would be arriving home soon—she hoped—and he would be pleased if things were clean.

"Home" was the tin shack. It was the only one she had known since she had married six years ago and had come to live on the research station at Sengua, where Clem was the officer–in–charge and chief warden. The shack had been built on unstable ground, and long before their arrival it had subsided, sunk to the point where it was impossible to close doors. For six years Meg had dealt with those open, uncloseable doors.

As she swept at the invading dust, she thought about those six years. They had not been easy ones, she would admit, They had been eventful, certainly, and far from dull; their three children, born here in the bush far from medical facilities, could attest to that. The years had taught her a great deal; survival in the wilderness of the remote African bush required that one learn to cope, for each day brought new hardships, new problems, new dangers to be faced and overcome. Mostly the years had been—she groped for the word—incredible, perhaps. She smiled and continued sweeping.

She remembered the night when, pregnant with their first child, she accompanied Clem on an anti–poaching patrol. He had left her sitting at the side of the lonely track while he dashed after two poachers they had stumbled on. She sat alone in the dark with a rifle across her knees, surrounded by the night sounds: the squeaks, rustlings, squeals, whines, snarls, roars, and howls of predator and prey; the sounds of the endless struggle for survival of the creatures of the bush. At the time, until Clem came for her at three a.m., the experience had seemed grim and terrifying. She smiled as she remembered how scared she had been. Now such episodes were taken in stride. She could no longer count the times she'd faced the dark bush by herself.

Her musings, and her sweeping, were interrupted by a full–grown female warthog, which dashed into the room through the open door. The warthog was followed at a more leisurely pace by an impala, a bushpig, and a dog. Established members of the household, they all found a spot to lie down, with the exception of the warthog. She came whimpering to Meg.

"McSweeney, what in the world?" Meg was startled to see that the hog's backside was badly blistered and burned. "You poor thing! You must have sat in the rubbish fire, you stupid piggy."

She hesitated a moment, then reached for the first aid kit. Working swiftly, she smeared the burns with aloe salve—she had made it herself from local wild plants—managed to get four aspirin down the hog's throat, and covered her with blankets to counteract the shock. McSweeney was then carefully placed in Meg's own bed. The warthog had often enjoyed this pleasure while a baby, sleeping at night with her adopted parents, but the arrival of other babies, both human and animal, had put an end to this practice. She snuggled in happily and went to sleep.

When the children came in later, Meg served them lunch, then set them to their daily chores. Clem did not arrive for lunch, sending a message that he'd been called out to inspect a leopard kill. He drove up in the truck shortly before sundown.

"Cheers, my darling," he said, giving her a bear hug and a kiss. "How goes the battle with your troupe?" And upon being informed of McSweeney's problems, he smiled affectionately and commented, "Well, if you must be earth mother to all the orphans in the bush, you must sort out the odd catastrophe now and then, I suppose." He looked at the warthog asleep in their bed and scratched his head. "Do I sleep on the couch tonight?"

"Not to worry," Meg laughed. "I'll fix her a bed of her own after dinner."

She looked at her husband, admiring his ruddy, out–of–doors complexion; sand–rust colored curly hair; and blue eyes with crinkles at the corners. He was rather handsome in a rugged way with corded muscles on a sturdy frame. He looks older than his thirty–two years, she thought.

Clem smiled back at her with his straightforward gaze. He saw a plainish woman, no makeup or cosmetics of any kind, with regular features and a pleasant visage. Her long brown hair was combed into an efficient bun. He wondered if someone meeting her for the first time would be able to tell how beautiful she had once been; if they would be able to see the beauty in the eyes behind the calm competence of the face. No matter, he thought, for *he* could.

He laughed, "Okay, Meg. No problem. Do what's necessary for McSweeney—she needs your attention right now."

For the next ten days Meg worked on McSweeney's burns. She awakened every four hours during the night to administer aspirin, fed her and kept the other animals from picking on her during the day. By the fourth week McSweeney had recovered. Her first move was to reestablish herself as boss of the menagerie. Meg's daily routine returned to normal.

The mail came from Ghokwe once a week, picked up and delivered by a game scout on a bicycle. It was their only contact with the world outside. Meg puzzled over the fact that though it took the scout two days to get to Ghokwe, he managed to make the return trip in one. When she asked Clem to explain this peculiar state of affairs, he replied, "You remember how traffic going into and coming from Makalipye works, my love? Traffic going in always gives way to the traffic coming from town."

"Yes, I've always wondered about that."

"It's because the people approaching town assume that everyone coming from town is completely smashed. Same for the game scout who picks up the mail. Booze lends wings to his bicycle, you might say. You may have noticed that he's not worth much for a day after he arrives back here."

"His cargo is worth its weight in gold," Meg retorted.

Clem looked thoughtful, rubbing his nose. He had marveled for years at this woman who had so cheerfully accepted his life in the bush, with no complaint of isolation, hardships, danger, and lack of comfort.

"Feeling a bit of cabin fever, Meg?"

"Not a bit of it," she replied. "It's just that I love to

get the letters from our friends in town." She walked over to the window and stood looking at the familiar scene: waxy green teak trees lined the banks of the soft–flowing river, and some baboons were sitting under them in the shade. Turning back to Clem, she smiled. "I love it here in the bush. I love the animals and the birds. The fact that I am the only white woman within one hundred fifty miles doesn't bother me in the slightest. I never think about it, actually. The times when we go out on population counts and live in tents with lions and elephants coming right into camp are special holidays for me." She went toward the kitchen to start dinner preparation. "And I shall hate to give it all up when you have become properly appreciated by the Department and are promoted to chief ecologist. We will all live in town in a proper house soon enough, my darling. The children will have proper schools, and I shall wear dresses. It will come, and I shall miss all this for the rest of my life."

One afternoon Meg realized that she hadn't seen McSweeney for a few days and wondered if she'd provided dinner for a leopard or perhaps some local lions. She was relieved to see her appear unharmed the next day, ravenous, obviously lactating and in what seemed to be a great hurry.

"Why, McSweeney," she said, " I do believe you've become a mother. Where are you hiding your new family?" A thorough search that afternoon failed to produce McSweeney's lair, but the warthog returned again the next day to be fed. This time when she hurried off after her meal, Meg followed, running to keep the little mother in sight as she trotted along. That evening she told Clem about McSweeney's surprising activities.

"She's bred with a wild warthog and has her litter hidden away in a proper warthog hole. I wonder if she will ever bring them here?"

"Shouldn't be surprised, luv." Clem smiled at his wife's concern. "When she's ready, of course. Until then she'll be showing up for rations only. Or she may actually revert to the wild and never come back. Hard to tell with wild orphans."

"Well, if she doesn't come back someday and returns to the bush, that's what we want, really. Isn't it?" Meg managed a smile in return. "I'll miss her, of course."

"You'll have others to take her place, Meg."

"No. She was the first. Nothing could take her place in my heart." Meg shook her head a bit wistfully.

She needn't have worried. McSweeney came every day for food and water. Then, as Clem had predicted, when she felt that her babies were old enough, she brought them in to meet her "family." To the surprise and delight of Clem and Meg, the babies were completely housebroken, and rapidly made themselves at home. Meg's menagerie now consisted of five warthogs, a dog, an impala, a bush pig, and three children.

It was not only the menagerie that was growing. The research station was getting larger, also. Meg watched, a bit resentfully, as the new shop and equipment yards were built, then the specimen warehouse and office buildings—all of good, substantial cement blocks, with slab floors and steel sash windows and doors. She said nothing to Clem, but he was aware of her feelings as he watched her somewhat futile efforts to make a home out of the crude tin shack.

"Hang on, Meg. I've put in for a proper house for us and should be getting an okay on it any day now."

"Don't they think we're as important as a lot of skulls and horns?" she inquired. Clem could only shake his head, not having a reasonable answer to her question.

They were both happy to see census time come, for this meant a month at Mana Pools on the banks of the Zambezi River. It was a time of hard work. The large-animal counts, along with all the other research on habitats, food and water supplies, disease, predation, and poaching, occupied the men's time from dawn to dark. But it was also a time of pleasant renewals of old friendships with other park personnel and their families: a day off now and then to go fishing when the airplane packed up and needed repairing; wonderful evenings camped together on the banks of the beautiful river; dinners with friends; beer drinking and tale-telling;

laughing and singing. The children played out each day to the fullest, happy for the opportunity to "go camping" on holiday, to live in the real safari tents in the midst of wildlife in unprecedented profusion. The women relaxed and gossiped, having only the meals to worry about and plenty of black help available at all times.

Meg wanted nothing to interfere with her view of the river, so Clem set up their two tents on the bank's edge under a huge *acacia albida* tree, a few yards distant from the tents of the other families. Here they had a semblance of privacy without any feeling of aloofness from the group. Most of the trees in the immediate area were *albidas*, and their pods were ripe and falling.

"We'll have lots of company in camp; the elephants love the pods," Meg told her children. "They have come here to eat them for many years; they will not be driven away by mere humans. When they come you must remember that we are the interlopers here, not they. They are gentle and won't harm us if we do not bother them. But Tembo doesn't appreciate being hassled. Give them all the room they seem to wish. Never yell at them or throw things at them, understand?"

The next morning, after breakfast was over, the two older children were helping clean up the dishes when the youngest ran up shouting at the top of his lungs, "elly!" and pointing. A lone bull was picking his ponderous way toward them, feeding on fallen pods as he came. They watched, eyes full of wonderment, as the immense grey body moved delicately among the trees, adeptly plucking pod after pod from the ground with his trunk and stuffing them into the huge maw underneath his tusks. Meg drew all three of the children close to her, and they quietly moved off to one side as the bull approached the tents.

"See how carefully he avoids the tent ropes? He will not touch one of them, he is so clever—even at night he will avoid them," she explained.

"Oh yes. They feed all night. It's cool then. They sleep during the day." Noting the apprehension on the childish faces, she smiled. "Don't worry. They won't bother the tents if you lie quietly."

The bull worked his way to the big tent which held the food supplies. He looked over the scene casually, then walked up to the tent door. Meg gasped, "Oh dear! I left the oranges out. I should have remembered!" The bull reached out his trunk, delicately picked an orange from the bag, and popped it into his mouth. He stood quietly, eyes half closed, and chewed slowly while he rocked back and forth, shifting his weight from one front leg to a back one.

"Ma, he's eating up our oranges!"

"I know, my darling. I know. With elephants, it's finders keepers."

The elephant picked out a second orange, then a

third, another and another; one at a time he ate every orange. He looked around—Meg was positive he wanted to make sure they were watching—then reached back and picked up the bag and ate that, too. Then, stomach rumbling audibly, he wandered on down the river bank and disappeared into the bush.

Six bulls made regular daily and nightly forays through camp, feeding. No tents, tent ropes, or clothes-lines were disturbed in any way, no humans touched. Soon the children were as fond of elephants as Meg had always been, but Meg saw to it that all the edible provisions were stowed away properly for the rest of their stay.

There were other visitors. One morning before sun up, two male lions went through the camp. It was gloriously exciting, especially when one of them stopped at a doorway of a neighboring tent and peered inside. The tent's occupant abruptly went *outside*, right through the rear end of the tent which had had no door until he did so.

Hyena were occasional visitors at night, looking for anything edible, even plastic or leather. Tent flaps were always secured at night against these rascals who would think nothing of snatching a bit of some sleeper's face with their powerful jaws. Twice a leopard went by the tents. Nearly every night there was at least one hippo in camp going or coming from its nightly feeding.

It was all wonderful, but the best of all for Meg was

the chance to talk to the wives of other Park officers. Even the most mundane of the events of their lives was, to her, novel, interesting. Conversely, they all found *her* life in the bush intriguing. Inevitably, the endless gossip and chitchat returned to the one common denominator of all their lives: the black man.

"The blacks believe that an elephant will return every year to the exact spot where it has killed a human. Not necessarily at the same time each year but some-time during each year." This came from Eva, wife of the local provincial warden.

"Last week," Eva said, "Graham was trying to get his plane out of some puddles on the strip. Three of his scouts were there, pushing very perfunctorily. You know how they always want to leave the really hard work to someone else. Anyway, since Graham figured that he was paying them, he told them, 'Dammit, if you're going to just lean against my aircraft and charge me for it, go lean on some other bugger's aircraft and charge *him* for it.'" The women all laughed.

"Typical, typical," Meg agreed. "Clem often gets so impatient with them. One of them will complain that something is too heavy to lift into the lorry, and Clem will grab it and throw it in himself with no trouble at all. Then the complainer just shrugs and says, 'Well, it's all those vitamins you eat.' It's really terrible, but it's funny all the same."

"They're all so superstitious it's unbelievable,"

Mary Cummings, wife of an ecologist, spoke up. "One of the men at Chawarwe suddenly decided that a spell had been cast on him, and he became totally blind. We tried to send him home, but he refused, claiming that his wife and father–in–law would use witchcraft to kill him. We had to take him to a nearby village which had a witchdoctor. The doctor cast out the spell and charged us fifty dollars. By the time we got home, the blind bloke was completely cured." More laughter.

"It pays to listen to them, though," Meg said. "It could save your life. Clem says that blacks have pulled him through several really bad scenes. Before we married, he was in Botswana and found himself in a drought area. He had two trackers with him and they were about to die of thirst when they came on a dry sand river. They dug in the sand where the elephants had been digging, and some water seeped up in the hole. Clem started to drink from it, but the trackers stopped him, saying that if he drank from the water, he would die. He told them that was nonsense, but they insisted again. 'White man die from this water.' 'But I can't go any further without water,' Clem told them. They repeated the warning. 'Only black African stomach can drink that water. We will drink. Then we will walk to other river for good water, which we will bring back to you in gourds.' He agreed finally—and a good thing he did. Local professional hunters told him later that the water of the sand river would have surely killed him. The trackers drank it with no ill effects, went for good water, and brought it back to him." She stopped, then added, "Even though they can be quite irritating, Clem and I have a good deal of respect for locals."

The four weeks of the animal count flew by—or so it seemed to Meg—and they found themselves back at Sengua. Their life was changing rapidly now. The guerilla war with the terrorists had broken out with a vengeance, and some of the patrols and stations came under violent attack. The land rovers were mine–proofed, the lorries armor–plated, and the officers and game scouts were issued automatic rifles and ammo belts. An airstrip was cut out of the bush alongside the research station; and men, supplies, and officials from headquarters came in and out rather regularly. Cement block homes were built for both officers and men—and their families. Meg was delighted, though it was neces-sary now for her to carry an F–N rifle everywhere she went. She was ecstatic over her new home. It actually had a kitchen and, marvel of marvels, a bathroom with a *tub*!

Along with these marvels came a villager to cook, do laundry, and care for the garden. He also cut wood and kept a fire going under the big boiler in the yard so there was always hot water. Meg could only count her blessings. If it took a war to bring about these miracles, then hurrah for the war. A few terrorists and land–mines were small potatoes in comparison.

With the expansion of the research station came new personnel, and soon Meg was no longer "the only white woman within one hundred and fifty miles." She gave up her solitude gladly.

Liz Martin was a relatively new bride. She was also new to the department, wildlife research, and the bush. Meg liked her immediately; Liz's determination and drive to learn everything about her new life intrigued her. Liz became fond of Meg and spent a good deal of time talking with her about the early days on the station. Walks and—when a vehicle was available—rides in the bush together became their favorite pastime.

"My God! My eyes are beginning to work like a bloody chameleon's—each of them going in a different direction," Liz exclaimed one day as they turned toward home after one of their rides. She rubbed her eyes and asked, "And you, Meg. How did you do it? Rowan told me that you had all three of your children right here. A bit rugged, wasn't it?"

"Not bad, Liz," Meg laughed; looking back she would not have changed any of it. "Clem scrounged up a pretty capable woman from the village to midwife, and he sort of supervised. After the first one, he was quite capable for the next two."

"God, what modesty. No drugs, no nothing."

Meg laughed again. "You do whatever you have to do in the bush, Liz. And you learn to do it for yourself. You don't last long otherwise." She was quiet for a moment, then added, "It was worth it—every minute of it."

"But why didn't you go into Salisbury?"

"We had no airstrip, no radio. No vehicles to spare. And Clem couldn't take much time from the station. You can't predict exactly when the little lovelies will arrive, you know. And, well, frankly, we couldn't afford to go. Clem wasn't making much money. We had to make do." She shrugged and laughed. "Nothing much has changed, only now we have more to make do *with*.

They drove in silence for several minutes before Meg spoke again.

"You know, Liz, giving birth to children under those crude circumstances was not the worst part of it. Far from being horrible, it was a rather special experience, with some lovely bits for me—and for Clem, too, I think. My love for the bush and what it has given me more than made up for the lack of proper medical facilities. I'd make that trade again any time.

"The worst problems were fighting the dirt and getting decent water to drink. I just couldn't keep anything clean, living in that tin shack, because the doors wouldn't close properly. And the only water we had was from the river. In the rainy season, it was always muddy and even if I boiled it, I always worried about it. There were times when we found fish in our tea!"

Meg laughed at the memory and wheeled the rover
into the driveway. McSweeney was lying in the yard,
waiting for her.

GERTRUDE

He walked through the door, not bothering to close it behind him. The afternoon heat lingered heavily outside the house, but it was even hotter inside. He went to a window, flinging it open. The house seemed to him like an animal, panting, mouth wide open to facilitate its breathing. He sat down, opened his shirt's top buttons, and slowly, without thinking, pushed his desert boots off. His mind was not really on the heat. He looked around the room carefully, trying to fix it in his mind—the way it was.

It was a beautiful room, he thought, the centerpiece of a beautiful house. Morey—the mailbox outside proclaimed the full name to be Moritz P. Thomson— had designed it himself and he was justifiably proud of it. His thoughts nibbled a bit at the fact that in his thinking he had used the word "house." Not "home." Ah, he smiled, how quickly the subconscious adjusts, accepting the change long before the conscious is wiling to face up to it completely. The fact amused him, interesting him long enough to take his mind off other things. Then the fact that he could concentrate on thoughts of human psychology and behavior on the evening before he was to lose this beautiful house occupied his wonder and added to his amusement. It was several minutes before he turned to thoughts of tomorrow and other days to come.

As he considered the uniqueness and absurdity of man—the animal—Morey was to a large extent unaware of the fact that he was himself not the best example to use as criteria for the mass of humanity. He was intelligent enough to realize that he exceeded the norm on that score, and interested enough in the study of his fellow human creatures to be aware of the vagaries and variety of human behavior, but he still assumed modestly that in spite of all the differences, he was still a pretty average sort of fellow. Which only serves to prove that most often the person one understands least is himself. Morey was many things. Average he was not.

He was handsome, in a quiet, blondish sort of way. His wavy hair, ruddy complexion and blue eyes formed a pleasing background for an engaging smile. A crinkle at the corners of his eyes held just a hint of inner amusement in their blue depths, and bespoke his appreciation of life's humorous aspects, by far the most interesting of which were those which applied directly to his own life. For instance, the current ones. The loss of his farm and his home, most of the nest egg provided by his wealthy South African father, and five years of his own labor and sweat.

Which reminded him of his own physical condition at the moment, and he decided something should be done about that. He headed for the bedroom, removing his shirt enroute. "Wonder where my *next* shower will be?" he mused. In the bedroom, the sun's rays were pouring through the western window at an angle so acute to the horizon that they became blinding. He stood facing eastward as he disrobed, his back to the sun. The all–glass east wall of the house encompassed both floors, so he could see the garden and maize fields that spread before him. A pleasant sight, the yellow stalks of the harvested corn tilting crazily, with the dark grey–blackness of the African veld peeking through here and there, all contrasting in striking fashion to the colorful pinks, reds and greens of the garden bougainvillea and rose bushes.

"It's beautiful; it's been pleasant here. I will miss it. I wonder how much?" His thoughts were almost casual, considering the circumstances. He picked a towel from the closet and walked into the large bathroom with its sunken tub and tiled shower. The water temperature regulated to his satisfaction, he stepped into the spray and began to soap. It was soothing to feel the warmth, the soft tattoo of the water droplets hitting his back and shoulders. It was a luxury that could prove scarce in his future; he did not hurry.

Finished, he pulled on clean shorts and shirt, tucked his feet into tennis shoes and wandered down to the bar to mix a drink. He could hear the cook and houseboy talking in the kitchen as they prepared dinner, the well–modulated murmur of their Bembe tongue musical to his inattentive ear. They were discussing the loss of the farm and their jobs, of course. Nothing much else had been discussed for the past two weeks, since he'd given them the unpleasant news. The other workers had left a week ago; Kari, the cook, and John, the houseboy, had stayed on to help him move. Most of the gear and equipment had already been stored in the barn on the new ranch; the balance would go with him tomorrow in his remaining vehicle, an ancient land rover pickup.

His father had been right. Damn him for that; he was always right; or at least positive that he was. No man should be right all the time, it made him impossible for other men to tolerate, full of arrogance and condescension. He was right enough to leave his native Scotland, emigrate to South Africa and make a hell of a lot of money, no argument about that. But somewhere along the way he had lost his only son. "Don't object to all the money, only object to all the rightness," Morey thought. "Rather like the money, one can do so much with it. Damned if I'll go beg him for anymore of it, though!"

Morey picked up his glass and tossed it down.

"Christ, how can I relate to someone who knows everything about everything?" The last time had really torn the ring out of it. The old man had been livid, had shouted at him,

"A *farmer*! In Zambia? You are out of your bloody mind! What do you know about farming?"

"I can learn, and I think I will like it."

"Ha! And what will you do, play symphony records to your cows? You will learn only how to throw away my money."

"It is my money now, father. I shall spend it as I see fit. And I think I'll raise pigs—not cows."

"Spend it, yes. You are good at that, spending money. My God, pigs."

"That's what money is for, really. Not just for making more money, which is what you use it for; but for spending. A man can be happy with it—or without it. But it should be only a means to some end, not become the end itself. Which it has been for you, father."

"You and your damn philosophy. You are thirty years old. You made a failure of your marriage and have no children, no career. When will you wake up and come live in the real world with the rest of us? You live in a world of books and music." The look on his father's face mirrored his profound distress, and Morey felt sorry for him as he replied, "Your world, the one you call 'real,' is the unreal one, to me, father. It is a world of money, credits and debits, buying and selling. Mine is a world of people, with their hungers and thirsts, happiness and sadness, feelings and emotions. It is a world of thoughts, wonders and doubts; of joy and grief; of music and laughter. You do not know this world, but most of the people who live on this planet live in my world, not yours."

"Do as you will, I cannot stop you. The money I gave you is yours, to make use of as you see fit." He shook his head. "I feel sorry for you, Moritz." There was a moment of silence between them. "But don't come to me for more when it's gone," he added.

"Hardly. And I am sorry for you, father."

Morey made himself another drink, drank from it and put the glass on the bar, stirring with his fingers again. That conversation with his father had occurred five years ago. He had not been a success as a farmer, not yet, anyway. Learning to farm was an expensive process, he had learned. Mistakes were costly. He had spent too much on his home, and nature had multiplied his problems with a drought the past two years. He'd run out of money. Saving what he could from the disaster, he had sold his equities for enough to buy a smaller acreage. There was no house on the new prop- erty, only a small barn and two metal grain bins. The previous owner had become discouraged and left Zambia to return to South Africa after hostile blacks had burned down the house some months before Morey bought the ranch. It would be quite a change. His next home would probably be a grain bin.

His musings were interrupted by loud squeals and grunts from the garden. What the hell? He ran from the house heading toward the source of the uproar. It became apparent that it was in or near the swimming pool. It turned out to be in.

"Good Lord, it's Gertrude!" he said to himself. Thrashing around wildly in the shallow end of the pool was a pig. More specifically, a 400–pound pregnant pig. Even more specifically, a thoroughly frightened 400–pound pregnant pig named Gertrude.

Morey shouted for John and Kari and cast about wildly for some inspiration as to how to get the huge sow out of her predicament. She was his best brood sow, and over the past four years she had also become a pet. He was quite fond of her. The situation was desperate when he reached the poolside. Gertrude could keep her head above water only by standing on her hind legs. She could swim, but because of her delicate condition, she was already too exhausted to make further effort. Her fright was rapidly disintegrating into total terror as the futile clawings of her front feet at the pool edge proved totally ineffective. Gertrude's stubby front legs had as much chance of pulling her vast bulk from that pool as a butterfly has of pulling an M–1 tank.

Morey did not hesitate at the poolside. He jumped in beside the floundering porker and began to shove and heave against her ample hams, hoping to give her the extra boost required. It was like pushing against a vast wall, and he gasped with the effort as his hands slid off the wet, writhing flanks and up her backside.

John arrived on the scene at this moment. To him it seemed that Morey was swabbing down—or up—the pig. A fact which came as no surprise to him, in as much as *nothing* his employer did could possibly surprise him, after the past five years.

He leapt into the pool without hesitation and began to rinse off the forward portion of Gertrude's anatomy, splashing water vigorously over her head and face. The poor pig could only surmise that this was an overt attempt to drown her even faster than she had expected to meet the end under her own efforts. Her struggles became accordingly more frantic.

Morey was trying to redirect John's efforts into more productive channels at the top of his voice, but was somewhat preoccupied with trying to keep Gertrude's flailing hind legs from turning him into a eunuch. The squealings and splashings made communicating pretty difficult. In desperation he staggered up to join John at the front end, grasped the lad's hands firmly and shook his own head slowly from side to side. John slowly realized that Morey was trying to tell him something, and stood quietly. Gertrude, completely exhausted now, quieted down, her front hooves clinging precariously to the dripping wet edge of the pool.

Morey explained the situation to John more clearly. "I'm trying to get her out of her, you jackass, not drown her. Now get up there and grab her legs and pull." He thought of something. "No, hang on. I'll get up there and pull. You get to the back end and push." No sense pushing his luck, and John could afford to lose more than he could.

They tried this system for a few minutes, but it was a total failure. Wet pigskin is a very slippery substance, and the more of Gertrude that came out of the water, the heavier she got. She wasn't able to help them, but her exhaustion kept her from hindering. Kari arrived now, a bit hysterical about the whole thing. Morey sent her to the other end of the pool for two inflated air mattresses, then to the equipment shed for some rope. The mattresses were lashed to each side of the pig. Then he and Kari pulled while John pushed.

Gertrude had apparently resigned herself to fate. She no longer struggled, limiting her activity to loud squeals and snorts. The extensive fear had taken its toll on her nervous system, however. The pool was suddenly awash with turbulence as escaping gasses made the water boil with the sound of a motor boat.

Morey collapsed onto the pool deck in laughter. John's discomfiture only made him laugh harder. Kari's disapproval was obvious. Finally regaining some composure, Morey expressed his admiration for Gertrude's efforts. "Wow! I've seen five thousand pound hippos that couldn't do much better than that. Cheer up, John. She'll be at least twenty pounds lighter now." And off he went again into uncontrolled laughter.

But the sow had to be saved. She—and her litter, if he could save them—represented a substantial portion of his worldly goods at this point. So they went back to the battle. Morey took two ropes and tied them to trees at the edge of the pool yard. He passed them under the pig, sideways, and had John get up on the bank to help. All three pulled on the ropes. Gertrude rolled up on her side, but they couldn't quite get her over the lip of the pool edge.

"We'll all pull on one rope together. Take the back one," he directed. This time the sow's rear end came over the edge. John hastily tied off the rope so that she wouldn't slip back, and they tugged on the front one. With a final heave, her front quarters cleared the edge. This rope was also secured, and they hurried to push her away from the edge. She lay quietly, looking like some weird monstrosity with the two air mattresses, and Morey sat beside her, rubbing and patting her head and neck, and talking quietly to calm her.

"She's in shock, John. I hope she doesn't miscarry. Put a rope on her neck so we can lead her to her pen when she feels like getting up."

"Okay, baas. I think Kari is in shock, too." He pointed to the cook, and Morey could see that he was right. She looked ready to faint, and her usual pristine white dress was filthy. In fact, as he looked more carefully, they were all remarkably filthy.

"Better lie down a bit, Kari," he said. "We'll finish here. Thanks for your help, and don't worry about dinner. We can make do until you feel better." Kari took to her bed for twenty–four hours.

After thirty minutes of quiet Gertrude regained her feet and headed for her pen with no urging. John bathed, dressed and served dinner to Morey after he had had a chance to clean himself up. Morey thought of the afternoon's events many times, and the memories never failed to bring laughter bubbling from his throat.

Will Gow drove into the driveway slowly, looking right and left. It was the first time he'd been to visit since Morey had lost his ranch and moved to this new place. He was curious, wondering what his eccentric friend might be up to. He pulled up and parked in what seemed to be the center of the farmyard: pig pens and feeders ahead and to the right, more feeders, a barn and two round metal grain bins to the left.

Nothing seemed to be moving in the afternoon heat. He could hear the metallic clang of feeder lids being dropped in some of the feeder sheds. A few of the pigs must be eating, in spite of summertime temperatures over one hundred degrees. But, there seemed to be no human life anywhere. The old pickup was parked by the barn, however. Will began to look around, called out, "Hey, anybody home?" A smile crossed his ruddy face as he looked around the yard. Neatness was not one of the words that came to his mind to describe it. "Home," indeed! He yelled again, louder. A door banged behind him and he swung around to see John coming from a feeder shed with empty feed bags in his hands. He smiled as he recognized Will, said, "Welcome, Baas."

"Hello, John. Is Morey here?"

"Yes, Baas. He is here somewhere. Perhaps he sleeps in the feeder there." He pointed to a shed on the other side of the yard.

"In the *feeder*?" Will was prepared for eccentricity, but this was a bit much.

"Yes, he often sleeps there when it is hot. It is cooler than the grain bin. Go through that door and call out."

Will headed for the shed, shaking his head. Opening the door, he poked his head in tentatively and called, feeling a bit foolish. It was a dark inside, and it was a moment before his eyes became accustomed to the dim light.

There was some movement from the bins on his right.

"Hi, Will." Morey was sitting up in a feeder bin, smiling a welcome.

"Hi, Morey. Thought I'd come over and see how you were making out."

"Glad you did." Morey climbed out of the bin and came to greet him, hand outstretched. "Come on, we'll

have a cup of tea, and you can inspect my new dig-
gings." Morey led the way to one of the grain bins. He
pushed the metal door open and held it for Will. It
creaked a bit. "Must remember to oil those hinges." As
far as Will could tell from the way that Morey was
acting, the grain bin might have been a mansion. He
walked in and looked around.

It was hot, not a breath of air leaked through the
corrugated walls. There were no windows, only the
squeaky door which opened to the outside. Sweat began
to run down his neck. Morey motioned to a well–used
easy chair, picked up a water jug and poured some into
a teapot, which he set on a Coleman stove. He pumped
up the stove, lit the burner and turned back to grin at
Will. Dragging up a straight–backed chair—as far as
Will could see the only chair there—he sat down and
asked, "How do you like my castle? Isn't it a kick?"

Will wasn't completely sure that he could appreciate
the humor of the situation, but he smiled and replied,
"All the comforts, Morey. A bit warm, perhaps."

"Yeah. The only drawback. It will be cooler this
winter." A chicken came through the half open door,
began to peck around on the floor. "Afternoons get too
hot for sleeping, so I take my kip in the feeder bins.
They're a lot cooler."

"How do you manage lying on the corn?" Will
asked.

"No problem. I lie on a blanket." The teapot began

to whistle, and Morey walked to the grain bin wall, picked up a five foot long one–by–twelve board and an empty nail keg. He set the keg between the two chairs and put the board on it. Then he rustled around in a big box and came up with two cups and one saucer, which he put on the board. "Sugar?" he asked. "'Fraid I don't have any milk." While awaiting the reply, he poured hot water in the two cups. The saucer went to his guest.

Will was so fascinated by the entire procedure that he forgot to answer the question. He noticed the inquiring look on his host's face, and hastened to reply, "No thanks, just plain tea." Morey found two tea bags in another box and dropped one in each cup. He sat down and grinned at Will, who was wondering what to stir his tea with—it was too hot to use his fingers. Morey pulled a sliver of wood from the edge of the board and gave his cup a stir, pulled out the tea bag and laid it on the board. "Stir?" he inquired, proffering the sliver of wood.

Will accepted the sliver solemnly. "Thanks," he said, and followed the example set by his host. He was beginning to wonder if perhaps there was something wrong with himself, and that all of this was perfectly normal. He looked at the rumpled cot. He pointed, "You sleep there?"

"Yeah, nights. John prefers the barn, but the rats kept me awake out there so I moved in here. I work nights a lot—it's cooler—and John takes care of things during the afternoons while I kip."

"I'm glad to see that he is still with you, Morey."

"He is good company, and he's loyal and honest. I don't know how much longer I can keep him, though. My money is getting awfully low. Wouldn't be right to keep him if I couldn't pay him, although he'd probably want to stay anyway."

"Why don't you write your father, or better yet go see him? He's got more money than he'll ever use. You can't go on living like this." He waved his hand vaguely around the bin.

"Oh, it's not so bad, Will. Really. I don't mind it at all—in fact, it amuses me." He looked at the raised eyebrows on his guest, and added to reassure him, "I've all my classical records and the stereo—we have some bloody fine concerts here some evenings—and every-thing I need for my own comfort. A bit short when it comes to entertaining my friends, I admit." He added the last ruefully, then perked up and shook his head with total determination. "I'll never ask the old man for another rand. Not a pence, Will. I'd take anything he offers—I'm not a complete idiot—but *ask* him? No thanks."

"Well, if you're not a complete idiot, you'll do until one comes along. Where's your bathroom? Tea always goes right through me."

"The longdrop, my friend, is just beyond the barn. The bathroom is still a figment."

150•

"A *what*?"

"A figment—of my imagination—a mere portion of a dream house that is so far little more than a scattering of scrawled lines on paper. It is a someday thing. From the way you are squirming, use the longdrop. You'll be much happier."

When Will returned, Morey asked if he would like a tour. The thought struck them both as hilarious. "You mean there's *more* than all this?" Will asked. "I'm under–whelmed. Wouldn't miss it for anything. Lead on, friend."

They looked at the feeders, the barn, the pigs. There was a good deal of joking and laughter between the two friends. Morey enjoyed a good laugh, even at himself.

They left the farmyard and Morey led the way down a short trail to the small stream that ran through a donga which traversed the ranch. They crossed the stream on some two–by–twelve planks and wound up the bank of the donga, still following the trail. It ended at a clearing which overlooked the water. Lava boulders protruded from the ground here and there, and laid out on the ground between three of the larger ones was a cement foundation.

"Well, I'll be damned!" Will said.

"No doubt. In the meantime, what do you think of the site?"

"Lovely. You've started your dream house, you rascal. The foundations are complete?"

"It's a start, anyway. I'll build it a room at a time, kitchen first."

"Why the kitchen?"

"To have running water for washing and a proper stove. It—the kitchen—will be big enough to sleep in while I build the rest. Next will be a proper bathroom with a shower." Morey's eyes sparkled as he spoke.

"No more kips in the corn? What a shame!"

"I may sneak over now and then, they might be cooler than the house in the summer."

A sound had awakened him. Morey lay on the cot trying to figure out what it was. Dawn was breaking over the veldt, he could see the greyness outside the grain bin through the open door. The strident territorial calls of the local doves were echoing through the acacias along the donga, as usual. He was used to hearing their symphony each morning, it never would have awakened him. It had to be something out of the ordinary. He lay there, puzzled but unperturbed, enjoying the birds as they announced the arrival of another day. He was clothed—more or less—except for his shoes. He had worked on the house the night before, and the nights were still too warm for bed clothing so he had kicked off his shoes and fallen on the cot without undressing.

He heard it again. A dull thump, followed by some loud grunts from the pens. He swung his legs over the cot edge, slipped his feet into his tennis shoes and ran out the door. Those grunts didn't sound at all normal. He didn't stop to tie shoestrings, the sounds struck him as desperate. He ran through the shed toward the stall he had prepared for Gertrude. How could she be having trouble, he wondered? It wasn't her first litter, and pigs don't usually have much trouble with births. The sow is large, and the piglet is so small that they usually just squirt out like melon seeds. The major risk is that the mother might squash one by lying on it.

He arrived at the stall a bit breathless to find John already there. It looked like John and the pig were having a wrestling match, with Gertrude winning. He could see piglets scattered around in the dried grass on the stall floor, crawling about blindly and squealing. They were not a pretty sight, the blood and fluids had not been licked away from them. He grabbed two of them up, found a box and stuffed them in it. Then the others, as fast as he could find and catch them up— seven in all—and turned to John and Gertrude.

They were something to see, he marveled even as he realized what the trouble was. Blood and excrement and uterine fluids covered the greater part of their bodies, glistening in the light of a lantern, and grass had adhered to the sticky fluids in splotches. It was a wondrous sight; Morey regretted there was not time to really appreciate it.

Two pink legs protruded from Gertrude's vagina. John had hold of them, trying to extricate the piglet.

Gertrude by now knew she was in mortal peril and was tossing herself and John about like a small earthquake. She was having a breach birth. There was no time to lose. Morey seized a stout rope and slipped it over her neck, made two fast half–hitches around a post with the other end, snubbing her up tight. The feel of the rope and the sound of Morey's voice calmed the sow; she'd fought ropes before and learned the uselessness. He stepped to John's side and ordered, "Hold her back legs as wide apart as you can, John." Then he took hold of the piglet's legs and tugged. Nothing, no give at all. He put his hand up alongside and felt into the uterus, hoping to turn the piglet. He couldn't tell exactly what was wrong, but it felt like the piglet must be crossways. There were legs inside sticking out from its body at right angles to the vaginal opening. He reached in further, his bare arm nearly to the shoulder.

"For Christ's sake!" he muttered, panting with the exertion. He'd felt two more legs. Was it twins, or Siamese twins? He felt around—only one head. He felt some more, counting. Four legs, inside! "Good Lord," he grunted. "It's a freak, John. That's why it won't come out." He pulled his arm out, sat back on his heels and considered. It had to come out, and damn quick. The piglet was probably dead already, suffocated. The problem was to save Gertrude.

Morey reached back inside, pulling the two crossed legs of the piglet in alongside its body and began working on the exposed legs, pulling and working them back and forth. The whole thing began to move and more and more of the piglet became exposed. He worked until four legs—the two extra legs were attached to the rear quarters of the baby—were visible, then took a new grip around all four at once. He looked up into John's grinning face, nodded optimistically, and pulled hard. There was a muffled "sluup" as the little body pulled loose, and Morey almost fell over backwards from the release of tension. John laughed with joy, and both of them gave a sigh of relief. Gertrude let out a long shuddering breath and two short snorts.

"That should be it, I didn't feel anything else in there," Morey said. "Take off the rope and see if you can get her up on her feet, John." He was still holding the piglet, though he'd almost forgotten it in concern for its mother. A sudden movement in his hand caught him by surprise.

"Hey, this thing's still alive," he said, astonished. Looking at it more closely, he was even more astonished. The piglet had four hind legs, all of them perfectly proportioned, as was the balance of its body. The extra legs and hams were between the other two normal hams, sticking straight behind. The piglet began to struggle. Morey gathered up the box with the first seven, put them all together and tendered them to Gertrude, who was now on her feet again and ready to begin her motherly duties. Methodically she began to clean them up, and they enthusiastically began to suckle.

"She may refuse to have anything to do with the deformed one," Morey told John. "He's almost sure to die right away anyhow, deformed animals usually do." They watched with interest, not even bothering to clean themselves. When Gertrude got around to the six–legged fellow, she hesitated. She seemed to think the whole thing over for a moment, then began to clean him.

"She takes him, Baas."

"Let's go clean up, John." Morey led the way down to the stream.

To the surprise of Morey and John, the deformed piglet did not die. It grew into an adult porker, but its life was not a very happy one. The other pigs were aware of its difference—the strangeness—and refused to have anything to do with it. Its litter mates ignored it or, even worse, treated it as a pariah. Only Gertrude liked it. She not only nourished her misshapen little offspring, she nurtured it with her compassionate company. Even in later life, after many other litters, she still treated it with understanding. Morey was always touched by the sight of the two of them together.

As the weeks passed, word of the amazing pig spread, and Morey was often visited by friends and strangers. The pig was a topic of considerable interest to John and Morey. It became a matter of convenience to give it a name, to avoid the constant reference to "it." John was enthusiastic in his support of "six–legs." Morey favored something not quite so graphic. It was his friend Will Gow who came up with the name that stuck, "The Beetle."

The Beetle's problems extended beyond the mere ostracism of his peer group. Each set of hind legs was complete and perfectly developed, up to and including a complete set of genital organs. These organs functioned perfectly, with the exception of minor problems due to the unorthodox location of those connected with the legs sticking straight out behind. However, the set located in the usual position of hind quarters were female; the other set were male. These latter were equipped with knees that would not flex, and stuck straight out behind. They were quite stiff, completely immovable. The legs which went to the ground were totally normal. The Beetle had no problems with mobility. But urination, or fornication?

It urinated through both sets of organs simultaneously. It was spectacular. The Beetle seemed bewildered by this phenomenon. The fornication matter was even more frustrating. Beetle seemed to have trouble deciding just which sex he–she was most of the time.

Morey spent some moments each day watching the antics of the confused hog. These moments never failed to leave him hanging limp and exhausted on the corral rail, tears of laughter in his eyes. When each mature sow came in heat Beetle would decide he was a boar and make futile attempts to mate with her. Pigs are mighty smart animals but not double jointed acrobats. The sows knew well enough what could and couldn't be done, and ran Beetle off, or ran off themselves, depending on respective sizes.

The high spot—or low, if you look at it from the viewpoint of the Beetle—was when her female organs came into season. That would damn near drive him–her crazy, along with most of the breeding boars in the pens. There was no way any of their male organs could reach the receptive female organs of the Beetle. But it certainly didn't stop them from trying—and trying. The endless troubles of the hog, its constant confusion, seemed extremely humorous, at first. But as Morey continued to watch, twinges of sympathy tugged at his heart. When the problem of dual gender became too much, Beetle turned to Gertrude, who never rejected her troubled offspring. To her the situation didn't seem all that funny.

The truck struggled up the hill, the motor lugged down under the load. Morey shouted to John, seated alongside, but the words were lost in the clatter of loose tappets and lifters, so he motioned to the door. John understood the meaning behind his gesture, opened the door and stepped off, running alongside to catch his balance, then leaned into the rear to push as best he could. It was just enough. Relieved of John's two hundred pounds, the truck took a new lease on life and chugged over the top. Morey kept it in low gear until John could catch up and jump in once more, then picked up speed, shifting up as the road dipped downhill toward the village. He turned to John, grinned and shook his head slightly, breathing a sigh of relief.

"Too many pigs, Baas," John laughed.

"Almost. I thought we weren't going to make it, for a minute there. We had to bring that many, though. Not much choice when you run out of money and food."

"Things are bad in the villages, too," John said. "It has been too long without rain, no one has enough to eat."

"Including our pigs, since we lost our maize, just like everyone else," Morey pointed out.

"We must live on bananas, Baas. There are still plenty bananas. The wild groves along the stream are thriving."

"Pigs, old friend, cannot live on bananas." Morey thought a moment. "Or maybe they can, I dunno. Never tried it." He laughed. "If we can live on them, I guess the pigs can too." He pulled up at the rear of the general store, which doubled as a butcher shop for the village. He left John to help with the unloading of the pigs and went into the office to settle up with the store owner, a Greek named Georgakopolus.

"Hi, Nick. I've brought you some pigs."

"Hello, Morey. They are unloading them in the pens

out back?" At Morey's affirmative nod he walked to the desk behind the counter and began rifling through some files. Finding the one he wanted, he walked back with it to the counter. "How many did you bring?"

"All the feeders that I had, Nick. Ten. I couldn't keep them anyway, we're out of feed."

"Ten? In that old crate of yours? I'll be damned." Nick laughed, and Morey joined in. "Well, here's your tab. You'll have a few Kwatcha coming after its paid off, with ten pigs."

"Good. By the time I get what we need, there may not be any left, though. We're out of everything. Do you want some help butchering the pigs?"

"No, we'll kill them one at a time, feed the rest. We can't keep meat fresh without refrigeration, as you know. We'll kill them as we sell them. What do you need—well, you know where everything is. I'll check on the unloading." He walked out back, and Morey began gathering his supplies. As he checked the items off on his shopping list, John came in.

"Baas, there are some people outside who wish to talk with you. Can you speak with them now, or shall I tell them to wait?"

"What do they want, John?"

"They have no food, no work, and their families are starving. They wish to speak to you of this, Baas."

"Tell them I will be out soon, John."

Nick came back, started tallying up Morey's purchases. When he had finished, he looked up. "I still owe you eighty Kwatcha, Morey. Do you want cash or credit?" He called one of his men to load the purchases into the truck.

"Credit, Nick. Not much use for money out in the bush." He turned to John and asked, "Did you clean out the truck?"

"Yes, Baas."

"All right, then. Where are these people who wish to speak to me?" He followed John outside. Five men were waiting in the shade of a mango tree. Morey walked to them, greeting them in their own language, Bembe. One of the men acted as spokesman for the group, "Good day, Baas. We are farmers who no longer have anything to farm. The rains did not come, and our corn is withered and dead. Our children have empty bellies, we no longer have mealies to eat."

"I am sorry, but I do not know what I can do to help. I have work, but I have no money and cannot pay you. Our crops, too, are withered and dead."

"Aiiiii." The groan came from five pairs of lips simultaneously.

"Baas." John came and spoke quietly to Morey. "There are many banana trees along the stream. Even if we give them to the pigs, we cannot use them all. There are wild mangoes in the bush near our ranch. These people are from my own village. They are good people. Can you let them live in the bush by the stream until the rains return?"

Morey stared at John in open–mouthed amazement. His astonishment gave way to a smile. "Why John, I'm surprised at you! I didn't realize you were so fluent, even in Bembe. That's the longest speech I ever heard you make." He looked at the men, scratched his head, looked down at the ground, stepped absentmindedly on a few clods. He turned his back and stared off at the brittle–dry blue sky. Far off he could hear the soft mournful call of an emerald–spotted dove. He recalled that the blacks believe the dove is saying: "My mother is dead, my children are dead, oh, oh, oh, oh." He swung around, spoke to the men.

"I will do this for you, if you wish it. You may come with your families and live in the bush on my ranch. There are bananas and mangoes to eat there, nothing else. You can work for me making bricks and help me build my house. When it is time for the rains to come, we will plant my farm together and grow the mealies. When they are grown, we will harvest them together. Then we will divide them into ten shares: one share to each of you, one for John and one for me. The other three shares go to the pigs. When you do not wish to continue this, you are free to go. What do you say to this?"

The five men huddled briefly, then their spokesman asked, "How long must we work each day, and must we work every day? Who will provide the seed for planting the mealies?"

"You work when I work. I have the seed," Morey replied, shortly. He had some doubts about this, but was willing to try it, for the sake of their wives and children. There was another conference and the men agreed to the proposal. It was better than starving. Morey told John, "They can camp on the downstream—not up-stream—side of us. Show them where to go when they manage to get moved."

"They will be there by tomorrow, Baas. There is little to move."

Morey put down the pencil and stared out the window. A chicken and a half–grown rooster wandered back and forth, pecking insects and crumbs from the floor, but he paid no attention. A huge pig snuffled a bit at the doorway, then came in and rubbed her rear ec-statically against the door frame. He looked at her and smiled.

"Gertrude, you old bag of blubber, cut that out!" The tone of his voice belied his words; only affection could be heard there. "I hope we can raise enough money soon to buy a door. This is like living in a zoo."

Morey was in the kitchen of the new house, which, with the bathroom, was all that had been completed so far. Some of the walls on the rest of the house were up, but the work was going slowly. The bricks were made by hand from the clay of termite mounds, and baked in Morey's own kiln. It took time, and the help from the villagers was far from enthusiastic. Morey didn't really blame them. Centuries of African tradition decreed that men should not work—work was for women—and the tradition was still strong in the more remote villages. Besides this, they had nothing to gain from this particular kind of work. Perhaps they would be more eager when they began planting the crops next week. Another problem was the matter of the current diet of the entire work force. Even Morey felt a bit listless these days, and tired easily. Bananas were not the best thing in the world to sustain energy, he found. He had been doing some calculations with his pencil.

"According to these figures, " he said to himself, "it takes fifteen banana–power to get one dobe brick in place on a wall." He had spent over a half–hour computing this scientific fact. "At this rate, if there are twenty thousand more bricks to put up, it will take us three hundred thousand banana–power to finish the walls." He looked at the figures with awe. "Whew!" he said out loud, startled by the magnificence of the concept. Then, thinking of seven of them consuming that many bananas—hmm, forty–five thousand each—he gagged and growled "yuk!"

He rose, walked to the door, paused a moment to scratch Gertrude behind her ears—a treat which she accepted calmly; her just due as queen of the farm—and then went to see what was holding up the next load of bricks.

"What's going on, John?" Morey was surprised to find them all in a huddle.

John left the others and came to Morey rubbing his kinky hair, a sure sign that he was uneasy. "They are not happy, Baas. They say they work for no pay to make you a great house, and they live in mud shacks."

"They were happy enough about the arrangement when their bellies were empty," Morey observed. "Well, they are free to leave anytime they wish."

"They do not wish to leave, Baas. They wish to share in the bricks, and to teach their wives and children how to make them, that they also may make brick homes for themselves."

"I'll be damned!" Morey was astonished. He turned this development over in his mind for several minutes. These men were not the usual black villager; they are willing to work—at their own pace, but at least they didn't expect their wives and children to do it all—and they seemed to have some moderate desires to improve their lot. Perhaps (his mind raced into overdrive) he could start something here. He was comfortable enough in his one–room mansion, the house would be done someday. Meanwhile a project with these fellows as a nucleus, then the entire village—God, the possibilities were almost unlimited!

He looked at the five of them, lolling in the shade; then at John. His mind snapped back into standard again. "Unlimited" seemed a bit farfetched, considering the "material," but there were *some* possibilities here. It was worth a try. He walked over to the men, John following.

"You wish to have homes made of bricks?" They nodded. "Very well. We shall start a new village down stream from my farm, farther than where you have your huts now. We will build a kiln and brickyard there; like this one, but bigger. You can clear land there for your own mealies. I will trade you chickens and pigs for your bricks after you have finished the first room in your new home. It will be much work, but I will help you as long as you do not become lazy."

The road had been first, so that the truck could come and go. The new kiln had presented no problem. They were surrounded by raw materials. The houses began to take shape; enthusiasm ran high. The word spread back to the old village, and new recruits appeared. These were promptly taught to make the bricks and lay them, so that they could begin their own houses. Meanwhile, bush was cleared and burned. The new village was taking shape in front of Morey's eyes. He was fascinated. And very busy.

He organized the children, taught them to plant the mangoes, bananas and citrus trees for each new house started. He worked with the women on the land clearing, teaching them to dig out and burn the old tree and brush roots, to keep the ground from souring. He worked with the newcomers, checking that the bricks were laid level and straight. He had never worked so hard. Each day was spent at the new village, after giving instructions to John who was left at the farm to care for the pigs.

Morey did not himself fully understand what was going on. He realized he was more involved—actually working harder—for the villagers than he had ever worked for himself. Just *why*, he wasn't sure. But whatever the reason, he was more motivated than he had ever been on his own behalf. He had to laugh. "Maybe it is all the God–damned bananas," he thought. "I must be drunk on banana juice."

One evening he arrived in the usual exhausted–but–happy state to find a visitor. It was his father. The greetings were a bit strained.

"Hello, father. A pleasant surprise to see you, but how did you find me?"

"It was not easy. The Greek merchant directed me. I arrived at mid–afternoon."

"Well, then you've had time to see everything. Come, we'll have some dinner."

"Yes," his father replied, "I've seen it all. Very impressive. One room completed in a half–built house, pigs and chickens walking in and out, dirty dishes in the sink, no furniture but a cot, two chairs and a stove. How can you live like this, Morey? You are not much better off than your pigs."

"You're partly right, father," Morey said cheerfully.

"But I am happy. More furniture, a big house, more clothes—these things would not make me happier, and anyway I can't afford them right now."

"You have no money, that's obvious. Are you telling me you wouldn't be happier with some money?"

"Well, it would be nice to have more money. For one thing I could offer you more than bananas for dinner," Morey laughed.

"For God's sake, Morey! Won't you please give up this craziness and come back to your own world—our world? You can have anything you want; all the music and books you wish. You should be associating with your own kind, not out here living with hogs and blacks." As his father was speaking, Gertrude poked her nose in the door, decided she had as much or more right there than this stranger, and walked into the room. She sat down and began rubbing her backside against the bricks in the wall. A look of sheer bliss spread across her face and she closed her eyes, the better to enjoy the luxury. The look on Morey's father's face had not the faintest connection with bliss.

"Ah, father, Gertrude has answered for me. She knows where she is happy, even though she is forced to live on a diet of bananas. And so do I."

ROGER

At eight p.m. we passed over the lights of Lusaka, capital of Zambia, and circled the airport for our landing. It was nine–thirty by the time we arrived at the hotel, registered and went to the bar for a coke. The hotel was a very nice hotel, for Africa. It felt good to relax after the tiresome flight and listen to Dave Ommoney, local manager for Zambia Safaris, outline our itinerary. As Dave spoke, a shortish man with heavy–lensed glasses came toward our table. He walked up and, disregarding Dave, shook hands with Elizabeth and myself.

"I'm Roger McKay; the *real* McKay," he laughed at his own joke. "I was in the tower when you landed, spelling the flight controller." He seemed proud of the fact that we had managed to land in one piece, as though he had been personally responsible. He turned to Dave and launched into a series of complaints, making suggestions for changes in Zambia Safari's operation that he seemed to feel were necessary. Dave nodded tolerantly, and smiled.

"We'll discuss it in the morning, Roger," he said patiently, and changed the subject.

I mentioned that I didn't have any local money; Roger instantly offered to cash some travelers checks for me and pulled out his wallet.

"Can you give me a check for the charter flight to Bangwelu Swamp?" he asked, adding "I need to rent the airplane right away to make sure we have it tied up."

I was surprised by his aggressiveness, but complied. He looked the check over carefully, holding it close to his thick glasses, picked up the travelers checks, said good night, turned and almost ran through the lobby into the night. I suppose I looked surprised because Dave chuckled and said, "Roger's a bit different, as you will find out when you hunt with him. He knows the swamp well, though. If anyone can find you a sitatunga, he can." He fiddled with his pipe, finally got it glowing again. "He's a good pilot too, claims he can fly anything up to and including four engine stuff."

I thought of the nervous, bumbly man who'd just left. "With those eyes? Can he see through those lenses?" It was an incredible thought.

"Does seem a bit surprising, doesn't it?" Dave says mildly. "He is an unusual chap."

That statement would have to be the understatement of all time. It would be some time before we learned this, however, because we were scheduled for other areas and other professional hunters for the first two weeks of our safari. The two weeks passed rapidly, as most time in Africa does, and it became time to drive to Mfue Airport to meet Roger and his rented airplane, a Piper Cherokee.

Roger was filling the gas tanks when we arrived. We loaded our gear while he finished and then took off for the Bangwelu Swamp hunting camp. Enroute Roger was talkative, and I learned that he had hunted with clients almost everywhere in Africa; that during the rainy season he drove an illegal taxicab in London, illegal because he had never been able to pass the physical exam on account of his eyes; that his wealthy British family had severed all connections with him; that his pilot's license was arranged with the help of a doctor friend in Kenya, whose ethics were below reproach; that he was an electrical genius; that no one in Zambia Safaris knew what they were doing except Roger, and that if they would take his advice he could have the organization operating shipshape in a week. I also learned that robbers had broken into Safari head-quarters in Lusaka and had stolen most of his equip-ment: radios, his big rifle, ammo, binoculars, and his prize possession, a stereo. Roger learned very little about Elizabeth and me. He didn't ask.

We found the grass–covered airstrip after a good bit of searching, while Roger talked to himself over his map about the fact that the "damned map must be wrong." A black lechwe herd of at least a thousand was grazing on the strip. We buzzed them and ran them off, but by the time we circled back to make our approach, a large flock of white cattle egrets had landed on the strip. Roger, muttering to himself all the while, landed anyway. They scattered in all directions. The sun was just going down behind the papyrus and reeds of the swamp when we climbed out of the plane.

We were greeted by a handsome young blond fellow named Robin Veal, who approached with a big friendly grin. He was greeted by a blast of critical comments from Roger about not having run the lechwe off the runway for us with his land rover. Robin good naturedly attempted to explain that the airstrip was four miles from camp, the plane was much faster than the rover, and he'd arrived just as we were landing, but Roger was not mollified.

"You should have been waiting for us," he said.

"Didn't know just when you were coming," Robin explained. "We didn't know until you buzzed the camp."

"Can't anyone do anything right in this outfit?" Roger growled and grumbled all the way to camp. When we arrived, he had a *real* fit. "This camp was supposed to be finished! Do you call this finished? What have you two been doing?"

We were joined by another good–looking young

man whose name was Andrew. He answered Roger with controlled civility,

"Working twelve hours a day. We arrived three days ago, and already have the clients' hut finished, the long drops done, and a start on the dining hut."

"No shower?" Roger sounded almost triumphant.

"It'll be finished tomorrow," Andrew was calm, but obviously angry.

Roger seemed to tire of the discussion. "I'll be in my tent," he said. "I've got to get my things arranged." With this enigmatic remark he stalked off in the gathering twilight.

"Would you folks like a cold drink?" Andrew smiled and waved us to some chairs. A fire crackled cheerfully before them. A table nearby held bottles and glasses. We sat, somewhat bewildered by what had been happening, and chatted with the two young men. They were graduate students from England, working for the summer with the safari company, camp–building at the moment, but most of the time working as guides on the company's wildlife walking–tours. Robin was a veterinarian, Andrew a biologist. They had the good taste to say nothing about Roger. Before our week with Roger was over, we would be grateful for their presence in camp.

Dinner was served under gas lanterns in the open, with a tarp strung on a line to fend off the night wind blowing sharp and cold from the swamps. Roger joined us as dinner was being served, complained that his radio wasn't picking up the BBC broadcasts, but said little else. None of us lingered after the meal. It was getting damned cold.

In the morning we got our first real look at camp. Robin was off somewhere with local villagers cutting reeds for thatch. Andrew was perched on the framework of what would become the dining hut, tying braces together with strips of bark. The cook came to inquire about our breakfast desire. He must have been seventy years old; even his wrinkles had wrinkles. I looked at his "kitchen." It consisted of two large boxes turned upside down that served as work tables, and a great clutter of food supplies lying scattered on the grass nearby. His stove was a great hole in the ground with a fire burning in it large enough to barbecue an ox. We opted for scrambled eggs and bacon. I could hardly wait to see how they would turn out.

Actually, the food wasn't bad at all. The old boy had done one hell of a job, considering his handicaps, and I told him so. Roger finally put in an appearance, said he'd been on the radio to headquarters. Seems that someone had forgotten to send up the Ag Cat—the special swamp vehicle—and we were going to have to wait for its arrival to hunt sitatunga. Meanwhile we would sight in my rifle and then go after a lechwe, as there was no meat in camp. Now I understood the spaghetti without meatballs we had for dinner.

Roger was wearing the same clothes he'd had on the day before; crumpled grey flannel slacks, white shirt, and black dress oxfords. This garb was not unusual for a plane ride, but it was the first time I'd ever been hunting in the African bush with a professional hunter decked out in this fashion. He looked weird with my binoculars—he had none of his own—hung around the collar of that white shirt.

When we returned with the lechwe, Andrew and Robin had finished the dining room and the shower, the cook had dug an oven in the sides of a termite mound. The camp had taken shape nicely, in our opinion. In Roger's opinion, as we were beginning to realize, nothing was ever satisfactory. He spent the remainder of the day screaming at the blacks, finding fault with everything. It was unbelievable. The four of us—Andrew, Robin, Elizabeth and I—were astonished.

"He's going to end up with a spear blade between his ribs if he keeps screaming at them that way," I said.

"Maybe not," Andrew replied. "I heard the blacks talking today about him. They think he is crazy, and they would never touch a mad man. They think he is a wizard, or sorcerer, in league with evil spirits." He was silent, lost in thought, for a moment. Then, "He's damn well going to get his nose mashed if he gives me any-more lip, though."

From the look on Robin's face I could see that he was in complete agreement. We all sympathized with the camp crew and trackers. They were catching it even when the blame properly should have been placed squarely on Roger himself and his state of general confusion. When he realized, for instance, that a special tool was not in the land rover, he screamed at the trackers, "Why didn't you put the tool in the vehicle? If you forget again I will *kill* you!"

The next day was much the same. We managed to shoot a Tsessebbe and Roger continued his row with the crew. His garb was still the rumpled slacks and white shirt. Elizabeth and I decided later that he hadn't changed them—or showered—for the entire week.

We were nonplused to find ourselves left to our own devices whenever we were in camp. Most professional hunters are embarrassingly solicitous of their clients, and though our two dozen safaris had long since ne- gated any need for special treatment, we did expect our existence to be acknowledged. But Roger headed for his tent or the cold box for a drink when we arrived in camp at the end of hunt, saying not a word. He didn't even offer us a cold drink.

On the third day Roger decided that the crew was stealing the sugar. He checked the sugar bowl on the dining table, then made the cook dig all the sugar out of the scattered supplies. He took it all and locked it in a trunk in his tent. Next he confiscated all the cigarettes, then the cokes. As a result we had to ask Roger when we wanted a cold drink, and Liz even had to ask Roger for *her* cigarettes, which he'd locked up in the trunk with his own. It was so weird it might have been funny if we had seen it happen on TV—to someone else.

That afternoon the cook asked Roger what he wanted prepared for dinner. Roger didn't answer—he was working on his damned radio, as usual. The cook suggested spaghetti, which we had for dinner on our arrival. This provoked a screaming lecture from Roger on the subject.

"A 'good safari camp' *never* serves a dish more often than once a week. *Never!*" He carried on for about fifteen minutes, growing more and more agitated as he warmed to his subject. I forget what we ended up eating that night for dinner, but I *do* remember what we had the next night. Spaghetti! Roger cooked it himself, to demonstrate another of his many talents. That was the fourth night.

Before dawn the next day Roger and I went to a spot "known only to Roger," where, he assured me, we would shoot a magnificent sitatunga. The day ranks number one on the list of horrible days I have ever experienced. Way out in front of the others. Roger neglected to tell me we'd be wading through sopping wet waist–high grass, so I left my waders in camp. He had remembered to bring *his* waders, however. It was cold, awfully cold, there was frost everywhere. Bengwelu is at 4,400 feet altitude, and it was winter. We tramped for three hours and thirty minutes, and I was drenched to my armpits for three hours and twenty–five of those minutes.

When we got back to the land rover—having seen nothing—Roger told the trackers to build a fire, so I could dry my wet clothes. He was quite dry, of course, and he went to the land rover and climbed into the cab. When I checked on him later he was asleep on the seat, using my down jacket for a pillow. I sat by the fire thinking the whole thing over a few minutes. Then I went to the rover, opened the door and woke Roger.

"I'm a little chilly, Roger, can I have my jacket, please?"

The sarcasm in my voice was lost on him, but he gave up the jacket, making no inquiry regarding my hunger, thirst, or general well–being. I went back to my seat at the fire. By one o'clock I was starving. I went back to the pickup; Roger was reading a book. I opened up the cab door, and asked,

"Is there anything to eat?"

"Oh yeah. There's some stuff in the coolcan over there. I forgot to tell you."

"What are we waiting here for?"

"We'll hunt this afternoon down along the marsh on the other side of the trail. No use starting until three–thirty." He went back to his book. Time passed slowly for me with nothing to do but wait, alone by the fire.

Ultimately Roger decided it was time to start out. We were going to drive for a mile or two, then start hunting. It was rough going, and quite boggy in spots. One spot looked *too* boggy, and I mentioned this fact to Roger. He drove through it as if he hadn't heard me. We barely made it, going downhill. The next bad spot was level. I knew the rover wouldn't make it, and suggested he go around. I might as well have been speaking Sanskrit. We got about twenty feet into the bog and the pickup went out of sight.

One look, and it was obvious we were in for a long afternoon. Roger started looking in the back of the vehicle for the hand–operated winch. After much frantic searching, he found it, but it was in pieces. No one had ever bothered to put it together. At five p.m. it was still in pieces. I mentioned to him that we were twelve miles from the nearest village, which was twenty miles from camp. Maybe something should be done about getting word to camp of our predicament? To my surprise Roger took my suggestion, and yelled for the head tracker.

"You are the one who is responsible for our trouble. This winch should have been put together in camp before it was put in the pickup. You were supposed to do it. You will walk to camp and get us some help."

The tracker protested. It was too far, and it was not his fault that the winch had not been ready to use. Roger started screaming, and the poor fellow headed off into the bush toward camp. Roger went back to the winch.

And I must give the devil his due. He was a good mechanic. He finally managed to assemble the device with all the springs, levers, and nuts in place, and the cable threaded through it. We pulled the cable out to dry ground and tied it around the spare tire, which we buried. We had just begun to work the winch when a group of blacks appeared out of the reeds and papyrus.

"Get your gun and load it," Roger said, "and stay up in the back of the pickup. Those guys could be dangerous." He continued to work on the winch while I kept an eye on the approaching men.

They were, we soon realized, a group of locals that our tracker had heard cutting wood on the other side of the marsh. He had convinced them to return with him to dig and push us out.

The winch did the job without help from the men, and as the sun started to disappear we were out on dry land. It was too late to think of hunting, we wearily headed back for the trail to the road. It was only a mile, but Roger managed to run the rover into trees twice, and get us stuck three times more before we reached the trail. Each time I warned him to go around, but he didn't listen. We arrived in camp about nine o'clock.

I got out of the car and said, "That was the worst day of my entire life, Roger. Thanks a lot. I'm all through hunting with you." The next morning I overheard him talking to headquarters on the radio. He told them, "My client is so unhappy he has quit hunting. It is all your fault for not getting the Ag Cat up here for us." Poor chap, nothing was ever his fault.

Next day Liz and I went with Andrew to the Bembe village to pick up some tea and cigarettes. The main road ran right through the middle of the town, brick houses on both sides for miles, no cross streets, no fences around the houses. Many small brown children ran out to wave at us, chickens and ducks scurried across the road before us and there were dozens of scruffy, barking dogs.

There was no store, as such, but assorted items were sold in some of the houses. We had to stop at three houses to find what we wanted. On the return trip, as we followed the meanderings of the dirt road between the houses, one of the ducks made a mistake. He under-estimated our speed and overestimated his own. His owner was very unhappy about this. In fact he was unhappy forty kwatcha–worth, about fifty bucks.

When we arrived back at camp, and told Roger he owed a Bembe villager forty kwatcha for a duck— which we didn't even get to keep—he was unhappy about five thousand buck's worth. He hollered and yelled for what seemed like a half–hour—at the villag-ers, at Andrew, at the duck. It was a pretty good display, even for Roger.

Shortly afterward, as I lay on my bed trying to nap, I smelled an unusual amount of smoke, and got up to investigate. I couldn't believe what I saw.

Roger was about seventy yards away, in the two–foot long dry grass that surrounded the camp, torching it. The afternoon breeze from the swamp fanned the flames and the fire spread rapidly; the camp was directly downwind.

The entire camp was made of dry thatch, a tinder box. "He's completely mad," I thought and headed for the kitchen area, yelling for the crew.

Andrew and Robin came running from their tent, and every one grabbed the nearest implement available and started beating at the flames. It was a warm, exhausting thirty minutes, but we got the fire out on the upwind side of camp. It raced on by camp on both sides, and we let it go. Nothing would be damaged now except the view. Roger was still running along beside the fire, flailing with a badly burned broom in one hand and carrying burning faggots in the other. We watched, unbelieving, incredulous. None of us will ever forget the sight of that man, in his dirty white shirt, crumpled grey slacks and black oxfords, dashing back and forth through the flames like a madman.

Conversation was not brisk that night at dinner. Roger had located some fishermen who lived in the swamp who were willing to take us in their dugouts along the channels into the interior, and he inquired if I was interested. It would be worth seeing, I decided, so we got up at four–thirty, ate some cold biscuits and took off in the land rover. We were to meet our guides at dawn near the airstrip.

For some mysterious reason, Roger decided to remove the cab from the rover—perhaps he thought we needed the fresh air—although the temperature was below freezing. We were skidding badly on the ice–covered mud, the wind hitting us in the face must have had a chill factor of ten below. Halfway to the strip, Roger threw the car into a sickening skid sideways, and we came to a stop headed the wrong way. To my amazement he shifted gears and kept right on going back down the road toward camp.

"What the hell are you doing?" I asked him.

"I forgot my shoes," he said.

"These are my best shoes. I can't wear them for wading in the swamp," he said. And back we went, hell bent for leather. We pulled up at his tent, he ran in, came out shortly, climbed into the car and off we went again, faster if possible. Boy, it was *cold*! I looked at his shoes. They were oxfords, same as the others, only more scruffy.

For two days we prowled around in that swamp, sometimes in the dugout, sometimes on foot. On foot it was a matter of slogging through murky, oily water between grass clumps that might or might not support one; there was no way to tell. It was impossible to guess how deep each foot would sink. Maybe to the knees, maybe up to the armpits. And Roger plodded along in his slacks and "used" oxfords. We saw a few female sitatunga, some lechwe, and a zillion marsh birds. It was so interesting I almost forgot I was with Roger. But not quite.

The seven days—somehow it seemed longer—came to an end. We were to take off for Lusaka after lunch. I knew Roger would have some little surprises saved for our final moments together, and he did not fail me.

At noon the Game Guard for the area showed up on his bicycle. He informed us that he was impounding the airplane. This, indeed, was the last straw. We *had* to take off by two o'clock to make Lusaka before dark, and our flight to the States was scheduled for that night. Seems that Roger had neglected to pay the forty kwatcha for the duck. He remained adamant, said he'd stay there a month but he wouldn't pay for a damned duck.

I took the Guard for a walk and talked to him carefully, using all my persuasive powers. He wouldn't take the money from me—neither would Roger. The Guard said he could file charges against us for taking pictures without a permit. It was a Mexican standoff. After an hour of earnest conversation I finally convinced the Guard to let us go. We loaded the gear on the plane while Roger put gas in the tanks. There was only one drum of aviation fuel, partly full, enough to fill the right tank about half–full. The left tank had about one–quarter left in it. Roger was, he said, "pretty sure there was enough petrol to make it to Lusaka."

Two and a half hours later, as we cruised through the haze, I watched the needle on the gas gauge for the right tank—we had been flying on that tank since takeoff—hit the peg. Roger made no move to switch tanks. I mentioned the matter to him.

"I never pay any attention to the gauges," he said. "I always fly by my watch. I know how many minutes of gas there is. We can fly for twenty minutes more on that tank."

I gritted my teeth. I could see myself creamed by a half–blind nut in a private plane because of his sheer stupidity. Ironical after having survived three and a half years as a Navy pilot in World War II. I breathed a sigh of relief when he finally switched to the left tank and we made it into Lusaka in time.

We were met by Davy Ommoney and an assistant and all headed in a car for safari headquarters. Roger sat in the back seat. Enroute, we ran into one of the police roadblocks that occur constantly in Zambia. The police-man questioned the driver, seemed satisfied that all was well and was about to wave us on when Roger started yelling at him. Dave turned around and said, "Roger, for Christ's sake, *shut up!*"

Roger subsided, protesting loudly that he "knew how to handle these blacks." The officer cast a hostile look in his direction. Dave hastily made the universal language gesture for "loco." We were allowed to pass through the barricade. At the headquarters, Roger took off into the darkening night. We never saw him again.

We did hear about him, however. When we next returned to Lusaka and Zambia Safaris I asked about him. Dave told me that he was no longer with the operation.

"After you left," Dave said, "he organized a group of five Italians for a bird hunt. They showed up with cases of wine and fancy cheeses and Roger took them to the Kafue marshes. There were no birds there, but, as usual, he wouldn't listen. There was no shooting, of course, so they all came back here and spent three days running about headquarters, shooting dicky birds and weavers and bee–eaters. Anything with feathers on it. It was an unholy mess. We threw the whole lot of Italians out and sent Roger packing. Don't know where his is now." Dave struck a match and put it in his pipe. It had gone out.

BANGUI

When I saw that the tickets indicated a scheduled stop at Tripoli, capital of Libya, on the flight from Paris to Bangui, no alarm bells rang in my head. It would not be necessary to change planes. A night flight; there wouldn't be anything to see except the lights of the airport. "We'll stay on board the plane and catch some sleep," I decided. Little did I know; Colonel Khadaffi had other plans.

The ancient Boeing 720 crawled up to the parking area and creaked to a stop, two of its jet engines whining for a long moment, then all quiet. Inside, there was the usual hubbub and bustle from passengers and cabin crew as those disembarking gathered their belongings and others stretched and moved about the cabin. Stewardesses stood by the cabin door waiting for the portable stair to be pushed into place. It seemed a long time coming. People stood in the aisles, impatient; the air began to become heavy. The grumbling started, questions were directed at cabin attendants, who seemed as puzzled as anyone else about the delay. The co–pilot came from the cockpit and conferred briefly with the chief steward. The intercom system clicked on.

"All passengers will disembark and proceed to the transit terminal immediately. Please remove all of your belongings and carry them with you." The message was in French, then repeated in English.

Surprised, with belongings hastily snatched together, we crowded down the aisles and through the cabin door into the night. Questions asked of the crew members brought only enigmatic Gaelic shrugs, and vaguely reassuring smiles. Everyone headed for the terminal building, dimly lighted, over a quarter of a mile away across the deserted tarmac. A hot, humid wind blew across us on its way from the desert to the sea, adding to our discomfort and depression.

Inside the terminal the lights were brighter, but the information was no better than it had been on the plane. We waited—and waited. Rumors and speculation were a dime a dozen. The snackbar ran out of anything cold and wet within ten minutes, and the coffee would have dissolved the enamel right off the cups, had they been other than paper. The entertainment was no better. It consisted of an endless harangue by various military types from TV consoles hanging above our heads—the fact that it was all in arabic only made it more ridiculous—almost funny in a tragic way—still going full blast an hour later when the loudpseaker suddenly came to life and instructed all of us to proceed back to the tarmac for "baggage inspection."

We trooped hopefully out into the hot, black night, headed toward our plane by unfriendly men with automatic rifles. By now extreme exhaustion was epidemic among us, and we reacted listlessly to the verbal proddings. As we drew near the big jet we could see the piles of baggage strewn around it, and armed men stationed everywhere we looked. Under the batteries of searchlights from military trucks, we were instructed to pick out our own luggage, move it into a line beneath the wings of the plane, and remain standing beside it. Feelings of helpless rage welled up within me as I struggled with the heavy duffle bag and suitcases, dragging them to the line. There was a look of fear frozen on my wife's face as she helped with the smaller stuff.

"What the hell is going on?" I wondered to myself, trying to smile reassuringly at her. We watched as fellow passengers were inspected, sent on to the stairway to board the plane. It was a slow process, and it became apparent that if you and your luggage were American, it was even slower. I began to wish we'd never heard of Central African Empire, or decided to go there for a fifteen day safari. Anyplace, America would have looked damned good to both of us right now.

A sudden outburst of shouting alerted us to a lone

woman standing with her luggage nearby. Four "inspectors" surrounded her, amid much arm waving and loud French. The uproar distracted our inspectors enough to make our own ordeal fairly perfunctory, and soon we were gratefully on our way up the stairs to the plane's cabin, where we would once again be in the hands of the French, thank God—free of the Libyan tormentors—and out of all the hassle. As we stood on the platform at the top of the stairs, I looked back. I was concerned about the woman, obviously an American, who had been the center of the big uproar. She was still standing with her luggage, guarded by a soldier, and crying into her handkerchief.

It was good to get back on board, a welcome relief from the fear we had felt while on Libyan soil. Though the plane itself was still on Libyan soil we felt safer, somehow. We watched the doorway, hoping to see the woman again, the woman of controversy. Who was she, and what had caused the problems? An hour went by, and more. At last we saw her coming through the door, helped to her seat by a stewardess. She was in shreds, tatters, almost on the point of collapse. Tear stains marked her face. Oblivious of the stir which her entry had caused, she sat in her seat and turned her head to cabin's wall, eyes closed. I asked a stewardess if she knew what had been the problem.

"Ah, M'sieur. She is the wife of the American Ambassador to the Central African Empire. The local authorities wished to make an example of her to embarrass your country."

The airport at Bangui was not exactly impressive. We headed for the terminal building with the others, hoping the safari outfitters would have someone there to meet us, in spite of our four–hour–late arrival. Inside the building we followed the signs—all in French, since CAE was part of French Equatorial Africa in colonial days—to Immigration, then to pick up our baggage and head for the examination tables of Customs. Most African nations are happy to see tourists and their money arrive, so Customs is perfunctory or nonexistent. Not so in Bangui.

Central African Empire—now Central African Republic—was one of the most impoverished nations in Africa. At the time of our arrival it was ruled by Bokassa, self–named "Emperor," and a cruel despot. Government employees had not been paid for nearly four months, people were starving to death, and a revolution was on the point of exploding. We were blissfully unaware of this as we sleepily approached Customs. To our surprise the officials were opening bags and actually examining the contents.

Our "examiner" was a corpulent black woman of surly mien who quite obviously had no fondness for whites. Elizabeth, my wife, proceeded through the line ahead of me, opening her traveling bag for the inspection as she arrived in front of the black woman. The latter rummaged through the bag, spotted a ballpoint pen and removed it.

"I take," she said, glaring belligerently. Liz opened her mouth, glanced at me and closed it again when she saw the slight negative shake of my head. The woman returned to her rummaging, coming up this time with a candy bar. "Ha! Very good. I take." Her expression spoke louder than words, "What are you going to do about it?" We said nothing, and with a long, pink and black forefinger she indicated we could proceed.

There was no one around the waiting room to pick us up. There were no taxis or buses—we learned later that fuel was almost nonexistent—and the downtown area was about fifteen miles from the airport. We waited, having no other choice.

Meanwhile, the ambassador's wife was going through Customs with her luggage. I was astonished to see that there seemed to be no one there to meet her or escort her through. She was treated as summarily as anyone else. This was not my idea of how American Ambassadors or their wives are normally treated, and the absence of anyone from the U.S. Embassy was unbelievable. Clearly the poor woman could not understand what was going on either. We had been in many African capitals in the course of more than two dozen safaris, and the past twenty hours was not what we had come to expect at the hands of Africans. Our treatment hadn't always been *good*, but it had never been this hostile. Also, U.S. diplomats and their families do receive good treatment, if for no other reason than all the millions of U.S. dollars that most African countries need in order to survive.

After a wait of some thirty minutes, cars began arriving in front of the terminal. Two of them were from the embassy, for the U.S. flag hung from fender–poles. The Ambassador's wife and her luggage were soon on their way to the city, and for the first time we saw a smile on her face. Our outfitter's driver was in one of the other cars, and we too were smiling as we drove towards town. It had been quite a trip, so far. Halfway to town we came upon the reason for the delay. A road-block had been set up by the CAE army, and all cars were being stopped and searched, their occupants interrogated at some length. Our driver explained:

"A revolutionary group put out a manifesto (hand-bills) declaring that if Bokassa hadn't resigned by the coming midnight, he was to be assassinated. The army is raising hell with everyone about it. Don't worry, this sort of thing happens here about once a month," he reassured us. At least he *thought* he was reassuring us. Liz and I were not so sure. The driver also gave us some of the facts of life in CAE as we waited our turn.

"Bokassa is quite mad, of course, and everyone knows this. He is so ruthless and cruel that everyone fears him. He never argues with anyone; he just has them killed if they disagree. He will listen only to the

French. He thinks he is another Napoleon. The French can get anything they wish from him."

"How do *you* people get along with Bokassa?" I asked, trying to make it sound casual. The outfitters with whom we were to hunt were Portuguese. We had hunted with them in Mozambique just two months before they had been exiled by the revolution, and found them to be dependable and knowledgeable.

"We get along fine, as long as we make money," he laughed. "Bokassa owns fifty percent of the Company."

"I hope business has been good," Liz said mildly.

The hotel—called the Rock for some reason—was a pleasant surprise after what we'd seen driving through the "suburbs," which had been a montage of abject poverty and despair. The central city proved to be mostly one–story, slightly–faded modern, some paved streets and sidewalks, even a signal light at the main intersection. It was not too impressive, and I had some misgivings regarding what Bangui's only—according to our driver—"real" hotel might be like. But it was quite nice, surrounded with colorful gardens, and located on the banks of the Ubangui river.[1] From the balcony of our room—when it wasn't too hot to go outside—we could watch the gigantic dugouts ferrying people back and forth across the river. There seemed to be a tremen-

---

[1] The Ubangi tribe was justly famous for the incredible stretched lips, like huge plates, that the women affected as a mark of great beauty.

dous amount of traffic, considering that the far side of the river was an entirely different country, Zaire.

We had been left to rest, after thirty hours of traveling, and told that we'd be flying out to the Kota river camp in the morning. We slept through most of the day, rising to take a short walk before sundown. The main road was lined with huge mango trees, some of them over fifty feet in height. The dirt sidewalks were covered with smashed and rotting fruit, and every tree had from two to eight people beating with long poles or throwing rocks at branches, trying to dislodge the remaining fruit still on the trees. With each newly fallen fruit, the ensuing scramble told us something of the condition of the local population.

When we arrived in the city center—perhaps six or seven blocks in extent—we noticed something else unique about the people. They were not only unusually black, they were also *very* French. It was most evident in the younger women. High heels and high fashion went hand in hand with starvation, apparently. We learned later that everything, almost, sold in Bangui is shipped in from France. When we returned to the hotel, night had fallen with the usual African suddenness. We walked through the lobby and up the stairs to our room.

"I've got to get some local money, Liz. The dining room expects to be paid in cash for all meals, it says here. I'll go back down to the desk while you get ready for dinner. Be right back."

She nodded, and I headed back down the hall for the stairs. Room phones or elevators were not part of the facilities. The cashier had just given me a handful of colorful paper and heavy coins for my traveler's check when the lights suddenly went out. All of them, everywhere in the entire hotel. Christ, but it was *dark*!

I waited for them to come back on. And waited. And more of the same. They didn't come back on. I had a problem: how does one find a strange room—I had only *been* to it once—in a strange hotel, when one can't see a damned thing? The answer came to me before I even found the stairs: you stumble a lot, and bump into many things you never dreamed were there. It must have taken twenty minutes, but I found the stairs at last, then the right floor, finally the room.

Inside I found something else: a nearly hysterical wife. Elizabeth had been in the midst of relieving herself when the lights went out. The bathroom was small at best, and in the pitch dark she couldn't find anything; her normal tendencies to claustrophobia went out of control. She finally fought her way out of the John, but there was no phone, she knew she couldn't find her way down to the lobby, and where the hell was I? It was a long, terrifying wait in the dark for her, imagining a million things that *might* have happened. So far it had been a great trip.

We made it through the night and back to the airport early the next morning to meet our pilot for the charter flight to the Kota River camp. He turned out to be a friendly young man of twenty–three with two very red eyeballs. During the three hour flight we learned what was causing the eye trouble: lack of sleep, the result of trying to keep up with the needs of five hunting camps almost totally supplied by air, and ten parties of hunters who had to be moved from camp to camp by air—with no apparent relief in sight (no pun intended), as he was the only pilot the safari outfitters had. He had been averaging about eight to ten hours a day in that plane. When I inquired how they managed to get enough time to run the airplane through the usual one hundred hour checks, he gave me a grim look and said, "Don't ask."

Our flight was uneventful, and we landed at the Kota strip shortly before noon, after buzzing the strip to drive off the waterbucks and kob. Moments later, arrived in camp, the pilot declined to join us for lunch, preferring to catch a short nap instead, before flying back to Bangui.

We spent six days at Kota camp. It was a clean, comfortable camp, the surrounding bush abounded with game—hartebeest, kob, roan, waterbuck, buffalo, lion, bushbuck, reedbuck, warthog, hippo—the hunting was ideal. Mornings always started out with the daily "radio call" to headquarters at six a.m., with two excitable Portuguese professional hunters screaming into the mike, "Ban–Ghee, Ban–Ghee" at the top of their lungs. It was an effective alarm clock. For two days our troubles seemed to be well behind us, and we enjoyed ourselves immensely. Then came day three.

We came in from the morning hunt to find the camp overrun with soldiers and policemen. The local District Commissioner, the district Chief of Police, four soldiers, and four of their "women", to be exact. All very black, all very arrogant. Luis Pedro, our hunter, dropped us off at the tin–roofed shack which was serving as our bedroom and went to meet the visitors. I watched, curious, from the window as the conference went on— and on—for most of the afternoon. About four p.m. Pedro came and explained what was going on.

"The government has not paid anyone for months, and the District officials are demanding that the safari company pay the trophy fees directly to them. They are desperate, with no income and starving, in no mood to accept "no" for an answer. I told them there was no money in camp, but that I would radio for some to be flown in. I have also invited the Commissioner and the Police Chief to have dinner with us. I'm sorry," he said, "but we'll need to handle them with kid gloves. You'll have to put up with them, we've no other choice. Hopefully they'll leave after dinner."

As it turned out, we put up with their two whores too, as all four of them came for dinner. The women were drunk, the two officials about half–drunk. It was a jolly party, as the fat, sweating Commissioner spent most of his time talking to Elizabeth, who couldn't understand his drunken English, and his girlfriend spent all of her time waving her arms around and talking loudly in French to no one in particular and everyone in general. I kept thinking it was some kind of bad dream. It has been eight years, but if I close my eyes and concentrate I can still see those eight cold yellow–brown eyes, no emotion showing in them, appraising us like cattle at auction, while they talked to us in French, then to each other in a native dialect. It was hot, the flamboyant multicolored shirts of the Police Chief and the Commissioner were soaked through. So was my khaki shirt, but for different reasons. The threat that hung in the air was so thick you could have painted a house with it.

The intruders did not leave until the next morning. Pedro gave them what meat we had in camp, and they climbed into their trucks and took off, telling Pedro they would "be back for the money." We went back to hunting, and no one spoke of it, but all three of us had our fingers crossed, hopeful that their return would be delayed until after our departure for Auck River, scheduled for day seven.

No such luck. Elizabeth and I were fast asleep in our post–lunch siesta on day five when the trucks roared back into camp. I jumped out from under the insect netting and ran to the window. No women this time, and more—twelve—soldiers. And they were quiet; cold sober. Pedro met them with a smile, but he was the only one smiling, I noticed. Quietly I told Elizabeth to stay in her cot, picked up the 375 and loaded it, sliding a round into the barrel and snapping on the safety. I eased back to the window and watched through the curtains, which were swinging gently in the hot breeze of mid–afternoon. I stayed carefully out of sight behind the window edge, wondering what would happen next.

There was a large lump of ice coagulated in my guts, and when the curtain happened to touch me I shivered from head to foot. I had never shot a man— even in WWII I had only shot at airplanes—but I knew, as certainly as I knew the sun rises in the east, that if anyone jumped Pedro, the Commissioner and Police Chief were going to be dead men.

I had to admire Pedro's coolness. He had no way of knowing that I was covering him, standing behind the curtains in my shorts and skivvy–shirt. He himself was unarmed and alone, facing fourteen angry blacks. I learned from him later that they had demanded the money, and when he told them it hadn't come from headquarters they demanded fuel, ammunition, food and guns. It was a lively row, to put it mildly, lasting about an hour and a half. Pedro handled it entirely alone. The gun–bearer and tracker were nowhere to be seen, along with Pedro's guns. In the end that was what swung the decision for us. As Pedro said later, "It's a damn good thing those bastards couldn't tell where you were, or where my chaps were, and weren't sure just what they were up against. They took the waterbuck and kob I offered them and said they'd be back for the money later."

As the trucks rumbled out of camp, I took a long breath and pulled on some pants, shoes and a shirt. Pedro sent his tracker trotting up the road behind the trucks to make sure they kept going, and we sat down to have a powwow. There was only one thing to be done, actually. We had to get the hell out of there; the next visit would be worse, and we all knew it. Somehow, Pedro got the plane in there by nine o'clock in the morning, and we were on our way to Auck camp twenty minutes later, arriving in time for lunch. It was the first meal in three days that I could taste.

This was a bigger camp with two other professional hunters and their clients. Located on the bank of the Auck River, which is the border between Chad and CAE, it is surrounded by dry, hot savannah that is part of the Sahel, a five hundred mile wide strip that runs completely across Africa. This entire area has suffered from drought for several decades, and is gradually turning into a southern extension of the Sahara Desert. It had no shortage of wildlife, despite the heat, because of the presence of the river, which is a good–sized stream year–round. There had been no problems with local officials, we were happy to learn. The heat sub-sided little or not all at night, which made sleeping difficult, but not nearly so difficult as we had found our last nights in the cooler climes of Kota. The heat seemed a mere trifle to contend with, compared to the Commissioner and his friends.

We relaxed and enjoyed ourselves. Elizabeth swam in the river, which was reported to be free of crocodiles at that point, below the bluff on which the camp was situated, in blissful disregard of Bilharzia and other water–carried African diseases. There was a sandy beach on the far side, in Chad territory, actually, where she enjoyed sunning herself. For two days. After that the river became off limits.

We could hear the staccato chatter of the automatic rifle–fire for some time before it dawned on us what it was. Pedro came from the radio shack to stand on the river bank alongside, as I watched Elizabeth swimming leisurely below in the river. He listened thoughtfully a moment, than called out, "Elizabeth! Get out of there and come here right *now*!" As she crawled out and started working her way up to us, he explained. "A new rebellion has broken out in Chad. That crackling noise is from automatic weapons."

Only hours later we saw the proof of his statement, as bedraggled and weeping refugees started crossing the river to our side with long–horned cattle and a few miserable possessions. For the remainder of our stay the shooting was often audible, and the stream of refugees never ended. At night we could see the fires burning.

On the fourth day at Auck camp the plane returned

with supplies, a passenger, and some startling news. The passenger was a Spanish nobleman whose name was Alfredo. He spoke no English—fortunately Pedro and I spoke Spanish—declared that he hadn't come to hunt, and that he only came to visit "his friends." He brought fancy cheeses of all types, and some nice wines, which he happily shared. He was a bit eccentric, or so it seemed to us, but a most welcome addition to our group. One of the other professionals, whose clients had left on the plane, talked Alfredo into going out with him that first afternoon to shoot a roan, loaning him a 458 for the purpose. Alfredo had never shot a rifle larger than a twenty–two, so our memories of him will always include the large patch–bandage on the upper bridge of his nose, a result of the one shot he fired. After which he rose to his feet, dusted off his hands and announced, "I have given up hunting for life. I do not like it." The professional picked up his rifle from where the recoil had flung it, and agreed that it might be a very good idea, indeed.

The news that came with the plane was the sort that puts a chill in the pit of your stomach. Pedro told me when Elizabeth was out of earshot.

"They've closed Kota camp for good," he said.

"Really! Because of the rows with the District officials?"

"No, it was worse than that. Even the Commissioner and his soldiers have cleared out on account of it. The day we flew out, our crew—tracker, skinner, gun bearer and driver—had nothing to do, so they went out looking for honey. They went down to the valley where we saw the lone elephant running away so fast that day. You remember?"

"Yeah. Where the big salt lick was with all the hartebeest."

"Right. Well," Pedro continued, "they ran right into a gang of poachers. A big gang, about twelve of them, with automatic weapons, walkie–talkies and four–wheel drive vehicles. The gang was poaching elephant and had about thirty–eight pairs of tusks collected. Been operating in that area for at least a week."

The hair on the back of my neck began to stand straight out. "What happened?" I asked.

"They were held for three hours and questioned about being part of the crew at the safari camp, which they denied," Pedro replied. "They said they were local villagers out hunting honey, and finally convinced the poachers of it, so were allowed to go. If there had been a white person with them, the poachers would have killed the lot. Damn near did anyway. Those well–organized gangs like that one come out of Sudan. They are usually Bedouins—you know, Dervishes—and just as soon kill you as look at you."

I knew, all right. They left no witnesses alive, that bunch. They'd smile as they slit your throat for the fillings in your teeth. I thought of our five days hunting the same area they were hunting, and how miraculous it was we hadn't bumped into them. If we had, it would have been our last bump. "No wonder we didn't see any other elephants," I said absentmindedly.

"Yeah," Pedro agreed. Neither of us was really thinking about the elephants.

I thought of all the "bad" luck we'd suffered through on the trip, and decided our luck had, overall, been pretty damned good, considering the possibilities. It continued good. I managed the animals I was interested in, and we were a happy camp. Alfredo turned out to be a whimsical, friendly fellow, one who was always doing something totally unexpected. Some days he roamed up and down the high bank on the river edge of camp, shooting with his twenty–two at any fish he might see. The fact that he never hit one didn't detract at all from his enjoyment; it only seemed to amuse him. Other days he went fishing for the huge Nile perch with local villagers, unconcerned with the audible war going on just beyond the far bank. He never caught any with his own gear, which was lucky. His pole and line were designed for trout or bass, and the two fish I saw caught from the river weighed in at over one hundred pounds each, and had been taken on an eight–inch–long hook tied to a rope, with a one pound chunk of meat for bait.

One morning one of the other professionals came in with a young tortoise—land turtle—about five inches long. He proudly declared his intention to keep the tortoise for a pet, and put it in a fair sized cardboard box and left the box in the corner of the mess hut when he went back out with his client after lunch. Pedro and Elizabeth were napping, and Alfredo and I were left sitting at the dining table, idly chatting. The tortoise was trying to get out of the box, which was a complete impossibility, because the cardboard was too slick, and his claws couldn't get any purchase. Anyway the sides were much too high. He didn't stop trying, however. We could hear the slow, measured "scritch, scritch" of his feet scraping the box, and it kept up without pause for almost two hours while we sat and talked.

Finally there was a lull in the conversation. The "scritches" seemed to get louder. I turned to look at the box. Alfredo also looked at it. Our eyes met, and there was a meeting of the minds.

"That turtle belongs in the bush," I said.

"Yes. And besides the noise is unpleasant," Alfredo said.

We rose, picked up the box, carried it two hundred feet into the bush beyond the edge of camp and released the tortoise. The scritching stopped, we returned the box to its corner, quite pleased with ourselves. It was pleasant to continue our conversation with the box silent. We could hardly wait for the professional to get back. Alfredo predicted he would blame the cook, and he was dead right. My already high respect for him went up a few more notches when the hunter returned, immediately came to the mess hut and looked in the box. Alfredo and I were sitting there solemn–faced— wouldn't have missed it for ten thousand dollars—to offer our condolences and wonder what *could* have happened? The hunter went through the thatched roof.

"The cook, the cook!" he screamed. "He has made a soup of my turtle! I will kill the son–of–a–bitch! I will kill him!" Alfredo never even twitched his face muscles, as the hunter ran for the kitchen.

At week's end we were once more in the plane headed for Bangui with Pedro and the pilot. Halfway there Elizabeth began to get sick. By the time we landed she was in the full throes of the Touristas, and barely made it to the safari headquarters before losing every- thing she'd eaten for the past three days. When things quieted down a bit in her insides, we went on to the hotel. Alfredo had insisted when we left him at Auck that we use his suite at the hotel while we awaited our flight home. It had not seemed very important at the time, but you never know about things like that—what might come in handy—especially in Africa. As it turned out, we were fortunate indeed.

We had been scheduled to fly out of Bangui the next day. Several things came up that made it impossible. For one, the airline cancelled the flight. For another, the safari company informed us that our passports, which had been left there for "safekeeping," had been turned over to the government immigration office for stamping—you must buy departure stamps—and that they had never been returned. And by now the visas had expired, which meant that we were *illegally* in the country, until such time as the government decided to extend the visas and give the passports back to us.

"Not as yet," the secretary smilingly informed us. "But I'm *sure* we'll have them for you tomorrow." Sure. Sure they would. I could cheerfully have killed the office force of the safari company for putting us in such a situation.

At any rate, we ended up in the fanciest—it had to be the fanciest, because it was the only—suite in the Rock Hotel, for three days. There were some lon–n–n–g moments when both of us feared we would "end up" there, or in jail, forever. It was a nice place to be sick, if you had to be sick, and Elizabeth definitely had. The first day she couldn't make it any further than the john, or maybe a better description of her movements would be to say she couldn't make it any further than her bed. Thank God there were two bathrooms—and two beds—in that suite. The second day she made it to the lobby. In fact we were sitting together on the only sofa in the lobby when the explosion occurred.

It was the first time I've ever been in the midst of an actual coup attempt. They can be quite noisy, and scary as hell. I would recommend almost *any* other activity, if you find yourself craving some excitement. The terrible thing about them is that everything is so out of control.

Because *everyone* is scared, I suppose. Both sides, the coup–ers and the coup–ees, and everyone else caught in between. It is not, however, dull. Not at all. Especially if you have no passport.

It was about two–thirty p.m., and I had just returned from my second futile trip to safari headquarters to see if our passports had surfaced, to find Elizabeth waiting wan–faced in the lobby. The sudden sound of sirens came from the center of the city, some six blocks away. All at once we were absolutely *alone* in that lobby. Every waiter, clerk and bellboy simply vanished, like magic. The men working in the gardens disappeared as though the ground had swallowed them. The cashier, the receptionist, gone. We didn't see them go, they just weren't there anymore. I glanced into the kitchen, bar and restaurant areas. All were deserted.

Then trucks, loaded with soldiers, began roaring by, seemingly in both directions. The drivers must have been making footprints in the floorboards; the trucks were going full–out, flank speed. Soldiers began to run through the grounds before the hotel, around the sides, finally through the lobby itself. We sat, there didn't seem to be anything else to do. Elizabeth was too weak to move very far, or very fast, and where in hell do you go?

Thirty minutes, more or less, after the whole thing started, a young black—not in uniform—followed by two soldiers stalked into the lobby, looked around and headed straight for us. He planted his feet and began to scream at me in French. Now, I have a good deal of trouble with ordinary french French, unless it's coming at me fairly slow. Bangui black French, screamed at me in a torrent, full of African idioms and colloquialisms might as well have been Ethiopian. I didn't have the slightest idea what he was saying, or why he was so obviously furious. It was apparent that he wasn't exactly handing me the key to the city, however. The tirade continued unabated, in spite of my constantly repeated "I do not understand, please speak more slowly"—in French—which he totally ignored. After at least fifteen minutes of this, he suddenly stopped, snapped an order at his soldiers and stalked back out of the hotel. To this day, I have no clue as to what it was all about. Maybe he'd been promised the Spaniard's suite for that night and was p.o.'d to find it still occupied. Thank God he didn't demand our passports.

The general uproar outside the hotel continued undiminished meanwhile, so we decided to try to get back to the room. We sat out the rest of the coup in our room, listening to the screams and shrieks. By six o'clock all was quiet. The coup had failed. The hotel staff was back at work, as though nothing had happened. Perhaps to the locals it *was* nothing.

The next day things were, as far as we could see, perfectly normal. Which is to say, pretty screwed up. The first thing we learned when we got to the safari headquarters was that their airplane, pilot, and two clients had failed to arrive at their destination; on the very next flight after ours! And no one had heard anything from them for thirty hours. As I was counting our blessings, the next thing I learned was that they still hadn't been able to get our passports back from the damned government. When I suggested to the manager of the Safari Company that perhaps the American Ambassador could help get us the passports back, he replied that the Ambassador had less influence than he did. I thought that one over, remembering that night at the Tripoli Airport, remembering that the Emperor himself owned fifty percent of the Safari Company, and decided he was correct. The day was not a total loss; I did manage to get our reservations confirmed by the airline for the following day's flight. If we could only get those damned passports before the plane took off.

The next morning Elizabeth and I camped in the Safari office. A clerk (black) was sent to the Ministry office at eight–thirty to pick up the passports, which were reportedly now available. She took one of the two cars. At nine–thirty the manager's assistant (black) was sent to find out why she hadn't returned. The plane was scheduled to take off at twelve noon. The airport was thirty minutes from the hotel, which contained our packed bags, and the hotel was ten minutes from the safari office. The manager's assistant had taken the remaining car. We were stranded, and the phone was not working that day. At eleven o'clock I gave up. Both of us were so low that we could have walked under a floor rug without ducking our heads. Elizabeth was barely holding back tears. At eleven–five a cheery, good–looking Frenchman drove up and came into the office, and we learned who really ran the country.

One look at our faces told him we were in trouble. We explained the seriousness of our problem. A moment's thought, a quick smile and he ran back out to his car, shouting, "I'll be right back, don't worry."

He was as good as his word. In ten minutes he was back with the passports, reporting that neither the clerk nor the assistant had been to the Ministry's office yet. "You can still make it. Pedro, you can take them in my car," he suggested.

Our spirits went up like a hot–air balloon with all the burners on full. We thanked him as we ran for the car, drove like crazy to get our luggage from the hotel and headed for the airport. Wonder of wonders, there were no roadblocks, and we arrived in time. We waved good-bye to Pedro as we climbed the stairway to the plane's cabin, and I noticed a tear on Elizabeth's cheek. But there was a smile on her face.

GRAHAM

"Down, man! Keep your head *down*, dammit!" Dennis was getting irritated. The rattle of automatic rifle fire added emphasis to his demands. A heavy whomp marked a mortar shell's explosion on the far side of the station. The two men burrowed deeper into the slit trench as the sibilant hiss of escaping gases warned them of an incoming rocket. It hit the cement–block house behind them with a deafening roar, opening it up like a 30–30 shell opens an old tomato can on the fence. Graham grabbed his left ear and moaned. Dennis had covered his ears when he heard the rocket coming.

"Thank God for the slit trenches," he said. "If we'd tried to defend from the houses we'd all be cooked potatoes now. What's the matter, Graham?" The man he addressed was older than Dennis' twenty–odd years. Forty, perhaps—it was hard to say. He was burned dark brown by constant exposure to the African sun, and his skin was hardened by outdoor living. At the moment he was digging at this left ear with one little finger.

"Damn! Bloody rocket blew too close. Can't hear a thing from this ear, Dennis." A lull in the firing gradually impressed itself upon their consciousness. Graham stood up in the trench and looked out toward the airstrip. "Wonder if my plane is still all right?"

"Get down, Graham, dammit. You're gonna get your head blown off over that precious airplane of yours." Dennis' words were hardly out when the momentary lull ended with renewed chatter from the automatics beyond the periphery fence. Graham, craning his neck in an effort to see the airstrip, paid no attention to the bullets flying around him. "Oh shit!" Dennis knew when he was licked. He took two quick steps and made a flying grab for Graham's legs.

"Unnh!" Graham grunted as they hit the sandy ground. He sat up, started poking at his ear again. "Bloody Tares," he said absentmindedly. "Hey, Dennis, I didn't realize you were such a jacked–up rugby player." A big grin spread across his usually placid face. "Maybe we can get up a game later, huh?"

Dennis' mouth opened, but no words came out. He stared at Graham, then looked down and began brushing sand off his shirt. "Yeah," he said finally.

Graham kept an eye on the gas gauge as he held the plane in a constant, shallow left bank in order to circle and follow the elephants. Keeping the herd in sight was no problem; eleven big bulls in full, panic–stricken flight through the mopane woodland were an obvious sight. The problem was to keep track of the one which had been darted when they split up, which should be any moment now. A six–inch sliver of white was not all that apparent as they ran through the bush five hundred feet below him. The gas, too, was a problem. He spoke into the mike in his left hand.

"I don't know if I can stick around up here much longer. I'm nearly out of gas now."

The reply came through his headset. "We'll never find him in this jesse[1] without you. Can't see twenty feet and tracks going every which way in the dry dust." The worry in Rowan's voice was obvious. The bull could die if they didn't find him to apply the antidote.

"I've got about five—maybe ten—minutes left. Maybe he'll go down before I have to scoot." Graham's voice was reassuringly calm. As he watched, two of the bulls turned away from the herd, heading east on an old game trail. He nosed the plane closer to them, checking. Yep! The dart was in the bigger one.

"He's turned off the big game trail about four hundred meters ahead of you, heading east. Got a smaller bull with him." Then, "He's slowing down, getting wobbly. Still on his feet, though. Watch out for

---

[1]Brush

his companion, he's running around in circles, looks pretty beady."[2]

Graham swung the plane back toward the ground party, spotted it running with Rowan and Tony in the lead, the others strung out behind. "You're about two hundred meters from him. He's standing still, but not going down."

The engine coughed twice, then caught again. He eased the throttle and headed for the bush strip.

"I've had it. Heading for the strip," he spoke into the mike matter of factly, busy calculating glide angles and distances to the tiny clearing. He needn't have told them. The plane was low enough so they all could hear it sputtering as it glided off out of sight behind the trees.

They raced on down the trail, concerned with the elephant. Graham could take care of himself; that was a fact of life for Parks Department personnel.

The engine sputtered a final gasp as the plane skimmed over the acacias and floated to the dirt runway, propeller windmilling. Graham climbed out when it stopped rolling, lit a cigarette and headed for the land rover parked at the side of the clearing. He could see two game scouts hastily getting it started, so he stopped where he was, and jumped in back with the gas drum when they pulled alongside. The rover jolted on to pull up at the plane, and the scouts began refilling its empty

---

[1]Angry

tanks. This finished, Graham started the plane's engine and taxied to the side of the strip, parked, and shut it down.

"I'm going to take the rover and see if I can't find the others," he told the scouts. "You can watch things here." Happy to return to their napping, they grinned their approval as he headed toward a narrow track that ran close to the game trail where he'd left the ground party and the elephant. Within fifteen minutes he had found them, still working on the bull. He left the rover in the trail, remarking to Rowan as he came up to them, "Thought you'd be finished by now. Have some trouble?"

"Yeah. That damned small companion wouldn't leave him, even after he finally went down. Kept us off for twenty minutes, running back and forth and raising hell. We must have fired off twenty rounds in the air, and yelled ourselves hoarse."

Graham nodded and proceeded to greet the other members of the party, most of whom were old friends. One young ranger was new, having been assigned to Wankie only six months before. He was introduced to Graham; John Duff.

He insisted on taking a picture of Graham, and was evidently very concerned with getting the entire affair on film. The terrorist activity was at its height, and everyone carried automatic rifles at all times; Graham was quietly amused watching Duff awkwardly trying to handle his rifle, camera, and statistic–gathering duties all at the same time.

A sudden cry rang out from one of the game scouts: "Mbogo! Mbogo!" Glancing up, they could see two old buffalo bulls trotting down the game trail toward them. As everyone else moved into the bush at the side to give the buffalo plenty of room, Graham was nonplused to have an automatic rifle shoved into his hand and hear Duff say, "Here, hold this and cover me."

Astonished to the point of speechlessness, he saw Duff walk *toward* the buffalo, camera at the ready. One of the buffalo turned off into the bush. The other's head came up, and his trot changed to a full run. Duff stood, sighting through the camera, as Graham and the others screamed warnings to him. Someone fired two shots in the air. Park's job is to protect animals, not shoot them, especially not for the sake of a photograph. Graham had moved to the far side of the land rover. Duff suddenly realized he was in big trouble, turned and ran.

The buffalo was gaining at every step, and it caught Duff and hooked him with one horn as they thundered past the rover. Duff flew through the air and landed sprawled across the still–drugged elephant's head. One tusk went through his lower thigh, pinning him to the elephant. The buff kept on going, disappeared around a bend in the trail. As everyone gathered around the torn and bleeding young ranger, who had to be removed before they could finish with the elephant, Graham thought to himself, "That's the first chap I ever saw get scragged by an elephant and a buffalo horn up his backside at the same time."

The three men sat on the shady porch, waiting for the waiter to bring the beer and sandwiches. David, the bearded one, asked, "What's happened to that bloke? It's been over a half–hour since we ordered." A bit of exasperation crept into his voice.

Ollie, oldest of the trio, replied, "Nothing, I should think. He and the cook are having a conversation, likely as not." With a nod of resignation he added, "There's no such thing as good service in any lodge since the war ended and the blacks took over."

Graham, his long–billed pilot's cap shoved to the back of his head, leaned back casually in his chair. "Relax, chaps. They'll get here eventually. I could sure do with a beer, though. It's bloody hot, even here in the shade." The dark blotches on the backs of the olive–green shirts sticking to their backs pointed up the truth of his words. He turned to Ollie, senior warden of the district. "Could you talk up a bit? You're on my bad side."

"Sure thing, Graham. Didn't realize you had one—a bad side. Can't you hear anything on that left side?"

Before Graham could answer, David laughed and said, "Only when he wants to. He hears me all right when we're radio tracking in his plane, even over the sound of the engine."

"I use my right ear for you, David." Then, to Ollie, "Don't hear much with my left ear. Wouldn't have it any other way. Couldn't stand being married for one thing. You've no idea how a deaf ear can prolong a marriage."

"Ha! Ollie learned your trick years ago, Graham. He's deaf in *both* ears." He turned, as the waiter appeared with three plates. "Good, here's the sandwiches. Hopefully, the beer will not be far behind." As they began to eat, he asked Graham, "What actually happened to Ranger Duff at Wankie? We heard he got ironed out by something and was in the hospital, but the stories were conflicting. Which was it? A buffalo or an elephant?"

"Both. A real crazy deal." Graham chewed rapidly, swallowed his mouthful, and continued. His listeners were quiet. Any tale from Graham was well worth the listening.

"This Duff chap was just assigned to fieldwork as a ranger about six months ago. He was a good, eager lad, with some ideas of becoming the world's greatest wildlife photographer. I had flown to Wankie to spot for them on some elephant darting. We finished up in a coupla days and were doing the last of them, actually. When the bull went down, I flew back to the strip and took the rover to drive into the site and watch them finish up.

"They were having trouble getting the radio collar

bolted together, but everything else had been done so I was about to drive back to the strip. Suddenly one of the scouts shouted 'Mbogo' and two old buffalo bulls came down the game trail. Duff was standing by me, and he handed me his F–N, said 'Cover me,' or something ridiculous like that, and started toward the bulls. Duff was peering through his camera at them, and I could see his lips moving but couldn't hear what he was saying. I guess he thought I was right behind him, but hell!—I was behind the jeep. I didn't want to get ironed out by a buff, and that one was sure as hell going to charge. Any damn fool could tell that.

"The buff broke into a run right at Duff, and we were all yelling, and I think somebody even fired a shot, but I'm not sure. Hell of a racket going on, and you know about my ears." Graham grinned. "Anyway, Duff finally realized he was in big trouble and turned to run toward us with the buff one jump behind and gaining."

Graham stopped and took a bit of sandwich. They waited while he chewed solemnly. Just as he was about to speak, the waiter returned with the beers. "Hey, the beer. Well done, well done," he said to the waiter. "Bring us another, please." He poured his beer in a glass and took a healthy gulp, licking the foam from his lips. "Super!"

His audience was becoming impatient.

"Dammit," David exploded, "will you get on with it? What happened to Duff? What was the damage?"

"Well, his camera was pretty badly knocked about. Doubt if it will ever be the same." Graham's face was perfectly straight. He watched David carefully, and when he thought the reddish hue of his neck was approaching the danger point, he added, "The buff hooked him, he flew through the air and landed on the tusk of the elephant. It went right through his upper thigh, in fact. Word from Wankie Hospital is he'll be okay in a few weeks. The camera has bought it, I think."

The full moon cast a beautiful, pale silver–blue glow over everything as far as they could see from the blind. The dead buffalo bait lay cabled to a stump, guts opened up, twenty yards in front. The mopane trees stood leafless like ghostly sentinels guarding the open space, some two hundred yards across, where they had chosen to set up the blind and bait for lion–darting. Winter drought lay heavy on the surviving bush. Lone territorial impala rams, in the height of their rut, snorted on their little knolls in every direction. Otherwise the night was silent. They had heard three male lions roaring moments before when the amplifiers had been broadcasting the jackal, hyena and lion feeding sounds, but the lions had stopped now that the recording had been turned off. There were four men in the blind. Three were awake, listening and watching. One slept.

"Where did you see him?" John Van de Meer, provincial warden in charge of the darting, whispered softly.

"I thought I saw him—only a shadow—over there about two hundred yards," Rowan whispered.

The third man readied his dart gun as they all watched intently for some movement out in the trees.

"Yes! See him there?" A shadow had slipped silently from one tree to another. The whispers became more excited; the shadow, appearing and disappearing, moved ever closer.

"He's awful spooky. We may not be able to use the lights." Rowan turned to Jack. "You many have to shoot him in the dark. I'll let you know."

"Okay."

The shadow had grown larger; became more distinct. As it reached the edge of the open ground, it disappeared. They waited for long moments, tense. It was pitch dark in the blind; the men could only see one another if silhouetted against the opening. They stood, nerves taut, waiting and watching, eyes strained against the dark.

A sound broke the silence—a strange sound that seemed to come from within the blind itself.

"What the—Oh, my God, it's Graham!" Rowan whispered. "He's snoring. Roll him over, or hit him, or *something*."

John felt his way quickly to the mats, tried rolling Graham on his side. The snoring continued; if anything, louder than before. John gave him a whack on the back of the head. Waking, Graham sat up, unsure of his surroundings, and started to say something. John's hand covered his mouth.

"For Chrissake, shut up, Graham." John hissed at him twice before he came wide awake and quieted.

Graham rolled off the mats and came to join them at the opening.

"He's gone. Scared him off with that infernal racket."

"You sure, Rowan?" John asked.

"Yeah. Saw him gap it."

"He may be back. Let's stay quiet for awhile."

"That's easy, if we can keep Graham from snoring."

"I'm going back to bed," Graham said. "If—*when*— I snore, hit me. It's what my wife does, and it stops me for a bit." He headed for the mats, and they could hear him lie down.

"We'll jolly well hit you all right, chum," Rowan said to himself grimly. "We're having enough trouble getting any lion darted, even without your damned snoring."

It was quiet for several minutes except for an occasional snort from a distant impala. A lion roared suddenly, not far off: compelling, rumbling up from his belly to shatter the night and send shivers up the spines of the watchers.

"That's him, no doubt," John whispered. The others were silent.

There was a small snuffle from Graham. John

leaned over, felt for Graham's shoulder, and hit it with a sharp blow with his fist. Graham gave a jerky gurgle and was quiet.

"He's coming. Out there," Jack whispered, pointing.

The shadow again, sliding from tree to tree, appeared for a brief second, then vanished completely for long moments, only to appear again, closer and closer. The lion stood in the shadow of the last tree at the edge of the open space, then slowly walked forward toward the bait. As he neared it, the moonlight came full on him. They could see the massive head and the mane, the huge muscled shoulders, the lean flank and long tail switching from side to side.

"Oh, wow!" Jack couldn't restrain a whisper of admiration.

"Shh! Not yet," Rowan admonished him.

The great cat lifted his head, and the roar filled the entire glade, startling the men with its loudness.

"Eeeorrrhunhh! Eeorunnh! Eeorunnh! Unhh, Unhh, unhh, unhh."

The men could see the belly draw up tight, the flanks shake as the roar rumbled out into the night. They were silent, enthralled with the beauty, the primeval wildness of the sight and sound.

The lion turned and looked for a long time at the blind, suspicious. It seemed that he was looking into their very souls. He turned back toward the buffalo, walked hesitantly around it. "He's not going to feed;

he's too nervous," John whispered in Jack's ear. "Get ready, and if you feel sure of your shot, try for him in the dark."

The cat turned broadside, walking away from the bait. He moved into the shadow of the big acacias under which they had positioned the blind and was not much more than a shadow once more. Jack followed him with the dart gun. In the black of the blind's interior, he could not see even the barrel of the gun, let alone the sights. The "feel" was good. He squeezed the trigger gently.

With the flat crack of the shot, the cat jumped sideways, the breath coming out of him in a startled "hunh!" as the dart buried itself in his shoulder. Graham left his mats in a startled leap and crashed hard into the blind walls. The cat whirled and ran, low to the ground, covering nearly ten yards with each bound. John swung the big torch, following the run until the cat disappeared around a combiatum clump a hundred and fifty yards off. The sequence took possibly five seconds.

"Sounded like a good hit, Jack. Good shooting in the dark," John said.

"How the hell does a man get any sleep around here?" Graham protested, stumbling over the recorder as he tried to orient himself. "All this fuss over a lion. Children, that's what you guys are, children," he muttered as he finally made it back to his mats. By the time the other three left in the rover to look for the lion—

twenty–five minutes, for the drug to be fully effective—
he was snoring again.

"I'll hit him when we get back here with the lion,"
John said, and they all laughed. They found the lion
about two hundred yards away.

There were two more lions that night, both lion-
esses. They proved quite simple, for they came in
separately and quietly began feeding at the bait. They
did not run when the big spotlights came on, and only
went about one hundred and fifty yards from the blind
before becoming immobile. John spent a good deal of
the night hitting Graham to stop his snoring. By daylight, they were all pretty tired, though happy with the
night's success.

Graham, wide awake at first light, said he felt okay
but had had a poor sleep. "My shoulder is awful sore,
too." He was puzzled by the silent glares he received
from his three companions.

To forestall other predators from making a meal out
of them, game scouts were assigned to watch the
drugged lions until they recovered and wandered off.
The four men then piled wearily into the rover and
headed for the research station and bed.

By four in the afternoon they were back at the blind
eating a combination lunch–dinner snack and chatting.
At dusk they would start the record player going, turn
the amplifiers on, and settle inside the blind for another
night's darting. Meanwhile they snacked and discussed

whatever came to mind. It wasn't long before the subject of Graham's snoring came up.

"I've done it ever since I can remember," Graham said. "I've become resigned to it. Been to three different doctors, asked them to operate, do anything at all. Told the buggers I'd pay any amount. It's horrible. You've no *idea* how bad it is."

"Oh, I think I've got a pretty good idea, all right," Rowan objected. "After all, we've worked and camped together for seven years."

"What did the docs say was causing your snoring?" Jack wanted to know. "Some kind of deviated septum or such?"

"The bloody buggers said there's nothing wrong with me at all—or if there is, they don't know what it is or what to do about it. Wouldn't operate—I begged 'em to do that—because they didn't know what to cut."

"You must have been a very popular fellow in the army during the war," John said dryly.

"Oh, very! Damn near got myself and a whole squad killed one night. The bloody Tares heard me. It came in handy once, though. I was camped out hunting crocs by myself. A lion came into the tent and pulled me right off the cot. I kept right on snoring; in fact I landed on my back, so the snoring must have been super. Guess he didn't care for it much. I woke up and saw the lion gaping it into the bush about a hundred yards away."

228•

"Nothing ever worked at all?"

"Yeah. One thing worked, but I couldn't stand it. One of those docs tried a tracheotomy tube on me. It stopped the snoring, but the tube whistled and I gagged all night."

"Ummm. Do you think you could stay awake all night tonight, old man?"

"Ummm. *No*, John."

"Ummm. Well think of something. We can't spend all night banging you again."

"I've an idea, John. It's not too pleasant, but it will keep the racket down." They watched with interest as Graham produced a roll of wide adhesive tape. He cut off a section with his skinning knife and parked it on one of the blind frame bars above the mats. "There. Before I drop off I'll pop that over my mouth." The other three collapsed. Graham had a triumphant grin on his brown face, a twinkle in his eye. "When it comes off in the morning, I'll not need to shave for two days."

The engine droned monotonously. Graham absently watched the ground stream by. He was not thinking about the bush below or the animals which his practiced eye automatically noted—the three bulls under the acacias; the cows and young working over the mopane thickets; the solitary black rhino sleeping in the combiatum; the leopard in the grass at the edge of the waterhole watching the impala herd drinking across the pond. Graham was thinking of Kariba, his home and the neighbors. As he thought, a smile spread across the lean, strong face, and he ended laughing out loud.

"I should have known better than to ask Mac about the dynamite," he mused to himself. "But he did such a hell of a job with the mortar on those Tares who jumped the fort at Mana Pools—sent the buggers running back to Zambia, those who could still run—I figured that he must know explosives. Anyhow, that bloody big rock had to go. It ruined the whole garden, and the new house I just finished building looked odd with it looming there in prehistoric splendor. Well, it's gone now, anyway."

A river appeared below, little water showing in dry season. He pulled back the throttle and eased the stick forward, dropping down to ground level and below, skimming over the sand bars and trickles, grinning as the reedbuck and impala dashed from under him toward the banks. He shoved the throttle forward, rolled the wheels of his landing gear on the sand, sprayed water over everything in sight. A laugh welled up in his throat as he really came alive. He was a part of the plane, or more correctly, the plane was a part of him. He flew it without thought, the way one walks, without conscious direction to the muscles from the brain. He pulled up after a few moments and headed back on course.

"Yep, the rock is gone," he thought. "Oh boy! Is it ever gone." The dynamite he'd used must have been about four times what was required. "There are parts of that rock that haven't landed yet, just went right on up into orbit." He was grinning again and laughing silently. "Hoo," he sighed. "The neighbors sure turned out to be a bunch of soreheads." Hell, he hadn't *tried* to bombard them with pieces of rock. Good thing he'd been called up to spot for the big cull and gotten the hell out of there. Maybe in a day or two they would cool off a little. My, but it was hard to believe—*seven* houses with holes in them. Wow!

A new noise in the engine's steady throbbing rang an alarm bell in his head. Instantly he was alert and automatically looking for some place to sit down as he worked the throttle and listened. Oil leak. The over thirty thousand hours in his log book said oil leak.

There! That clearing. He could set it down there okay. Might be close getting it off again, though. The plane banked and slipped sideways, sliding down toward the clearing. He cut the ignition—mustn't score the cylinders. The wind sound through the struts, the muted "plup, plup, plup" of the windmilling prop sounded forlorn to him. It had been more than two years since his last forced landing. He came into the clearing, slipping wing–down into the crosswind, nose up, rudder pressure holding it from dropping. Just as the tail was about to hit, he released the rudder. The nose came down and swung left, the plane straightening out as the front and rear wheels hit the ground together. The plane was through flying as it hit—stalled out. He hadn't touched the flaps. It rolled fifty or sixty feet and stopped.

He got out and matter of factly lit a cigarette as he studied the clearing. If he tipped it on its side and went between those two trees he could make it, maybe. Well, worry about that later. First, find the leak.

He jerked the cowling, began to search. Nothing this side. He walked around to the other, climbed up on a strut to look over the top of the engine. "Ouch! Damn, that's still *hot*!" He sucked the burned spot. Nothing here either. He bent to search lower. Aha! It was a line. He wiped it with a cloth to clean it and look more closely. A swivel fitting had cracked, and the oil oozed out through the broken threads. Graham went back to the cabin, poked around in his tool box.

This oughta do it, he thought, and picked up a fitting, a spanner and easy–out. In ten minutes he had the line fixed and new oil in the engine to replace what he'd lost. He wiped up, put the cowling back and buttoned it down. *Now* we'll see about getting out, he thought. He was whistling, actually happy to have this unexpected problem to stimulate him—a break in the routine. Ha! Routine was no word for flying in the African Bush. The unexpected problems *were* the routine here.

He walked over the clearing, planning his takeoff run, clearing the ground a bit where he could. It was rough enough; he hoped the tires would take it—and the struts. He walked back, smoked a cigarette, and considered.

He had a choice: a hell of a long, hot walk or try it. When he had considered everything, he decided he could make it. If he hadn't been sure, he would have walked. He believed in the old adage—there are old pilots and there are bold pilots, but there are no old, bold pilots—which was why he had over thirty thousand hours flying in the bush.

He got in, fastened up, and kicked it over, feeding in the ignition and gas. The engine caught. He revved up to 1500 and left it running there until it was warm, checked out, and sounded good to him. Then he turned and bounced back to the very edge of the clearing, turned again, and put on the brakes. He shoved the throttle full ahead, held the brakes as long as he could and let it go. It bounced, rolled, bounced and gradually picked up speed.

The end of the clearing was coming too fast. Graham shoved the stick forward, then pulled back, trying to get the wheels off the ground. It bounced into the air, settled back, bounced again, settled a bit, then staggered up—slowly, so goddamned slowly. Graham was whistling through clenched teeth. The trees came at him, too high to clear, too close together to go flying through level. He waited to the last second, shoved the stick to the right, away from the wind, and gave it full left rudder. The plane hung on its side for an instant—just long enough—and he was through between them. He snapped the plane level again, picked up speed, and climbed up to clear the next ones. Slowly his jaws came unclenched, the whistling stopped. He pulled out a cigarette and lit it, headed for Mana Pools again.

"By God," he muttered, "if we get finished early today, I'm gonna land on a sandbar on the way back down the Zambezi and do some fishing."

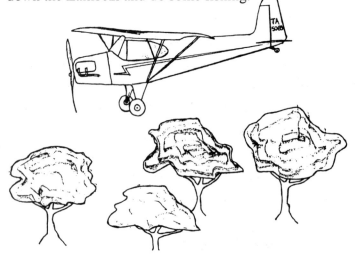

THE FISHERMAN

The others were already in camp, he noticed as he clambered over the grey granite boulders that lined the banks of the river, heading for the flat shelf on which they had set up their sleeping bags that morning. Thousands of years of winters' rushing torrents had deposited enough sand there to form the only flat spot for two miles in either direction up and down the river. On that four mile stretch, if sleeping lying down was part of the plan, the gravel bar was the place—the only place.

His companions greeted him with wide grins. One of them handed him an opened beer can as he placed his fly rod against a convenient tree and sat down on a rock in the shade, sighing a tired "Thanks." The other asked, "How'd you do?"

"Not bad, caught lots of rainbows, no browns. You guys keep enough for breakfast?" As they nodded, he grinned suddenly and said, "You won't believe this."

"Oh no," they groaned almost in unison, "here it

comes."

"Really, I'm serious," he said. "Damndest thing that ever happened to me. I caught a deer on a fly!"

"You *what*? God, your stories get worse every trip."

"No kidding, I really did. I caught a deer on a fly."

"Bullshit, old buddy. Your stories are always hard to believe, but this one is just plain impossible."

He protested and swore oaths of honesty, but to little avail. His two friends laughed at such a ludicrous tale, one suggesting he's been too long in the sun without a hat this afternoon. His patient insistence began at last to wear them down, and a demand finally came for more details of his incredible feat. He enjoyed their puzzlement, telling them just enough to keep them guessing.

"Well, I have to admit that it wasn't legal. It wasn't even a buck, it was a doe—full grown doe. Hooked her right behind the ear. I was using a Rawlins' special number 10 at the…

"For Christ sake, cut that out!" Fred mimicked his voice, "I was using a Rawlins' special—what kind of baloney are you handing us?"

"No baloney at all, Fred. Every damn word I've told you is the gospel truth, so help me. *Really.*"

"So what did you do with it?" Jim inquired skeptically.

"Turned it loose, of course. It wasn't legal, and it's not even deer season." He was quiet a moment, then, "I wonder if they have a special season for deer fishing

236•

with fly rods, like they do for archery..."

"Damn you, Rawlins," Jim exploded, "what the hell is going on? What, if anything, really happened?"

The fisherman was having trouble now keeping a straight face, but he smiled innocently and answered, "I *told* you that you wouldn't believe it."

"And we sure as hell don't, but you might as well finish so we can start getting some dinner together." This from Fred.

"That's about all there is to it; I was false casting to dry my fly, had a lot of line out, and hooked this deer behind the ear. She wasn't a keeper, so I slipped the fly out of her ear and released her."

"Jesus! For ten years I've been listening to your weird stories every time we go hunting or fishing; but this takes the cake." Fred was smiling, but Jim was a bit irritated. "You just slipped the fly out of her ear?"

"Yeah, no trouble."

"Sure. And where did this miracle occur?"

"About three quarters of a mile downstream."

"The deer was on the bank?" Jim was intrigued in spite of his doubts.

"No, she was in the water, behind a log."

"Just standing there, watching you?"

"No, not exactly." His companions sensed that the whole truth was not far off now, and began to question pell–mell, like hounds on a hot scent.

"How'd you get her to hold still—why didn't she

run off and break your line—did you really pull the fly from her ear—they came too fast for him to answer, and he laughed. The look that passed between his friends was obvious—"it's all a big damn lie!"

"Hold on," he said, laughing again. "Everything I've told you is the exact literal truth. It really is. But not the *whole* truth. Even that is still pretty unusual. The thing I didn't tell you was that the doe was dead. Drowned. Lying in the water half submerged behind a log. I never saw her at all, accidentally stuck my fly in her ear on a backcast, and thought I was hung up in the damn log until I went back to extricate my fly. Truth, my friends, is often stranger than fiction."

Fred laughed, Jim shook his head, muttered "God save us, two more days of this."

They started dinner, Fred and the fisherman amused by Jim's continual monologue of mutterings.

"Brings us sixty miles back into this rocky gorge, last eleven miles down the side of a precipice, over a road that's so rough and impossible that we spend more time on the hillsides winching over logs and through snowbanks than we do on the road—hell, there *isn't* any road most places, and where there is it's straight up—then he goes off fishing, comes back with no fish and a fish story to end all fish stories. Why do I come on these crazy trips?"

"Must be the stories, Jim," Fred grinned. "It sure couldn't be the camp–spot or the road in." He ducked the loaf of bread that Jim threw, laughing as he retrieved it to the table.

They managed, between joking and sips of iced whiskey, to put the dinner together, the lanterns casting grotesque shadows into the darkness around the fire as they moved about. All of them were hungry, and the steak and roasted potatoes, corn and salad were pleasantly satisfying. As the heat from the canyon walls diminished, jackets were donned and the folding chairs moved closer, the fire stoked up with fresh wood, now that the coals were no longer needed for cooking. A coyote yipped a quavering call and another answered. The echoes in the canyon multiplied the effect into a complete chorus which slowly died away, as the men listened, silent and appreciative.

"Beautiful," breathed the storyteller, a note of awe in his voice. "We're probably the only humans who heard that—maybe the only ones within fifteen miles of this place." An owl hooted softly, the sweet low call of a screech owl, scarcely heard above the constant background of the churning waters so close behind them. "A real wilderness symphony, you'll be sung to sleep tonight."

"I don't think Jim was planning to sleep tonight," Fred said. "Just going to worry about that nonexistent road all night."

"No way, big brother—no way. I'll be in dreamland five minutes after the dishes are done. Gonna sleep all night, fish all day, and in between eat fish in the morning, drink booze and eat steak at night. We'll get out of here the way we got in—by the grace of our guardian angel and the luck of our sterling leader, teller of tall tales, the man who fly fishes for big game." Jim picked up the kettle from the grill, poured hot water into the dishpan, added soap; poured the balance in another pot for rinsing. "Let's have 'em fellahs."

Twenty minutes later the camp was quiet, except for the thin crackle of the dying fire. The brothers were asleep almost as they hit their sleeping bags, placed side by side on the ground on one side of the fire. Their older companion had put his bag, along with a spotlight and his duffle, on the other side, spread out across the floor and tailgate of the jeep wagon. He was in no hurry to sleep. His head was out on the tailgate, where he could look up at the stars. He smiled as the comfortable sound of snoring came from the other two, amused again by the memory of their reactions to his tale.

God, the stars were gorgeous, he thought. Always so much bigger and closer up here in the high woods where the air was cleaner and thinner. The rustle of the night wind in the great yellow pines growing on the canyon walls combined with the sharper murmur of the river's rushing waters nearby and the distant roar of rapids above and below the bar—all together a soothing, hypnotic song, one he never tired of hearing. "What a lovely world this is," he thought, but by then he was asleep.

A noise entered his dream world—a different noise. It troubled him because it did not belong there, and knowing this he awoke. Lying still, wondering why he had awakened, he heard it. It was a small noise, perhaps a squirrel or rat. He reached for the spotlight. Rolled over onto his elbows and pressed the button. The brilliant beam lighted the entire camp area, and the cause of the noise was most apparent. A brown bear was sampling a loaf of bread left on the table. It had been the crackling of the bread wrapper that he'd heard, not the bear. He marveled at the total silence of the animal's movements, even as he considered his course of action.

It was a large bear, of the black species, and paid not the slightest heed to the spotlight. It was between the jeep and the two sleeping bags on the ground with their blissfully unaware occupants, perhaps twelve feet from them.

They didn't have enough food to share it with a bear, not if they were to stay the trip planned out. The only firearm of any kind in camp was his twenty–two pistol, at the moment resting in the duffle by his side. It would be totally useless against an animal this size, but as a last resort, it might frighten him off if fired in the air. The man decided to try something less violent first, however, realizing that any normal bear should be easily frightened.

He picked up one of his shoes and tossed it. The

effect was nonexistent. The bear didn't seem to mind a bit, continued his consumption of the bread, at a rate of about three sandwiches per bite. The man reached into the duffle for his pistol.

"One shot should do it," he thought to himself, and climbing from his bag for more freedom of movement, he pointed the gun skyward and pulled the trigger. The effect left something to be desired. The bear raised his head and looked—for the first time—at the spotlight, then returned his attention to the remains of the bread.

"I'll be damned," the man thought, "I'd better move that son–of–a–bitch, one of the guys will jump up from his bag any second right in front of a scared bear—or an unscared bear—the noise of this gun sounds like a cannon in the still of the night." He fired three more shots from the automatic as fast as he could pull the trigger. The bear jumped about six feet from the table and stopped, swaying his head from side to side, look-ing at the light, and sniffing the air.

He was closer now to the man—no more than ten feet—and he looked bigger than ever. "Damn that bear," the man muttered, "why won't he get the hell out?" The possibility of rabies suddenly occurred to him, and he aimed the pistol at the ground under the bear's feet. It was crisis time; this was his last hope, to spray the bear with dirt and sand. He fired twice into the ground, and was relieved to see the bear turn and run ponderously from camp. He glanced at the other sleeping bags.

Fred was sitting up, eyes wide open, and inquired calmly, "What's going on?" Jim was sound asleep still, and the man couldn't believe it. Six shots fired within twenty–five feet and it didn't even wake him up. He answered Fred.

"A bear was in camp. I couldn't scare him off, so I sprayed him with dirt and he finally ran." Fred asked a few more questions quietly, was apparently satisfied with the answers, and lay back down in his bag. The spotlight was turned off after the pistol was reloaded, and the camp became quiet once more. Soon all were asleep. It had been nearly one o'clock, the man noted.

Again it came, awakening him. "Damn," he muttered, switching on the spotlight, sure that the bear had returned. He was pleasantly surprised to see not the bear, but a three point buck, still in the velvet. He watched, fascinated, as the beautiful animal minced its delicate way by the table, picked a fallen lettuce leaf from the ground, and daintily walked right between the sleeping men on the ground while munching its treat. Neither sleeper wakened, and the spotlight was switched off, the man watching the deer move slowly off, feeding as it went, in the moonlight. It was three a.m. He rolled over and went back to sleep.

Dawn found him awake, and as he pulled on his clothes, Fred awoke, sat up, looked over at Jim, still asleep.

"Morning, Fred. Sleep well?"

"Like a top. Hey, Jim! Wake up." He gave the bag a shake with his foot, bringing his brother crawling out in a hurry. The fisherman finished his dressing, said, "Fred, will you throw me my shoe over here, please? It's over there past the table."

"What's your shoe doing over here?" Fred asked as he picked it up and brought it to the jeep.

"Threw it at the bear. I was trying to 'shoe' him out of camp."

"I'll ignore the lousy pun, what bear?"

"The same one you asked me about last night, pal. How many bears do you think came in here in one night?"

Fred looked puzzled. "You mean there was a bear here last night?"

Now it was the fisherman who looked puzzled. "Dammit, Fred, we already discussed this last night at some length. You were wide awake talking to me about that bear for ten minutes."

"No way." Fred shook his head. "I slept straight through. This one I won't buy—"

"He probably hooked it with a #10 special," Jim offered.

"Hold it a minute, fellows—who's telling tales now? I know damn well we discussed that blinking bear last night." He walked over toward the table, carefully studied the ground around it. "Come here, you two nonbelievers." He pointed to the tracks, then to the half–

chewed loaf of bread, then led them to the jeep and showed them the empty shells from the pistol. "Well?"

Fred looked confused. "There was a bear here all right. But I sure don't remember even waking up. When was it?"

"About one a.m. I fired four shots, and he hardly moved, so I shot at the ground and splattered him a bit, then he ran off. You sat up in your sack and we talked it over for several minutes. Jim never woke up at all— slept right through it. Then about three a.m. a nice three point buck walked through camp, feeding. He walked right between your sleeping bags."

Jim looked at the ground by his bag, said softly, "I'll be damned." He turned to Fred and reminded him that he sometimes spoke to people at night, then couldn't remember it the next day. The look of frustrated bewilderment on his brother's face made him laugh. He turned to the fisherman. "From now on you can tell me that black is white, old friend. I'll believe anything. Let's eat and go fishing."

As the eggs were sputtering in the bacon grease a sudden gust of wind swirled through camp, scattering dust and ashes. "You'll find some eggs under these ashes," Fred assured them as he served up the breakfast. "Damned wind fucked them up."

"It may be worse for the fishing than for the eggs, if it gets any stronger. Think I'll take a bait rig along, just in case."

The brothers, full of optimism, took only their fly rods and headed upstream for the crossing. The fisherman dug around to find a spinning reel and put it in his jacket, then headed down the trail as the first rays of sunlight broached the canyon depths and reflected sparkles from the rocks on the far bank of the river. As he walked he kept an eye on the big pines and white firs above him on the hillsides. "It's picking up, getting stronger," he thought. The trail brought him back into the river a mile downstream. He put his fly rod and reel together and selected a salmon fly imitation with large white bucktail from his kit. The wind was ruffling the surface by now, and he wanted something both he and the trout could see. He worked his way into the water and began casting upstream.

In the first hour he caught and released three small rainbows, decided to change to a grasshopper pattern. The fish were now refusing to rise to his fly on the surface, and he began fishing it wet, catching two more, one of which he kept as the hook had been in such an awkward place that the fish was exhausted before he could remove it. The wind was whipping badly now. Leaves and dead sticks littered the water and casting had become very difficult. He sat down on a convenient rock and considered, eating an apple as he rested.

He knew the fish would be feeding on the bottom now, picking up goodies from the debris knocked into the river by the wind. Time to change. He put the spinning reel in place, attached shot and hook, and went to the closest riffle. Wading in the shallows, he kept turning rocks slowly, trying not to muddy the water. Several times he made sudden grabs at something on the bottom side of a rock. About one grab out of three he was quick enough to succeed. He found some moss, wet it and put it in a jacket pocket, placing the insects he caught carefully under the moss. He started back downstream, stopping only at the big pools, tossing the weighted hellgrammite into the foam at the head of the pool and letting it settle with the current.

A most unsatisfactory way to fish. There was only one thing he could say for it—it was one hell of a lot better than not fishing at all, at least for him. One problem was that he could not release them all, some were hooked too deep. By two o'clock he had enough, and headed for the trail back to camp. When he arrived in camp, he found his friends already there, discussing—more accurately cussing—the poor fishing. He fish safely in the coolcase, he joined them.

"It was actually dangerous," Fred was saying. "A couple of those gusts dropped dead limbs near me that were big enough to kill a man."

"The casting was the dangerous part" Jim said. "I hit myself in the forehead right between the eyes on one backcast. Damned hook went clear to the bone. It took Fred's pliers to pull it out." He rubbed the spot tentatively, with gentle care, and winced a bit. "How did it go with you, deer catcher?"

"I gave up on the flies after an hour or so. There was so much shit hitting the water that I couldn't see a fish take, and it would have been a mighty foolhardy fish to get up near the surface in that rain of debris. Fished for awhile with hellgrammites. Caught one nice brown— about twenty inches or a bit more—go maybe four pounds." At the quizzical looks he added mildly, "He's in the coolbox. I knew you wouldn't believe it if you didn't see it. We'll barbecue him for dinner. Split down the back, skin intact to hold in the juices, covered with salt, pepper and lemon butter sauce." He tasted it mentally, nodding his head.

"And dust," Fred said.

"And ashes," Jim added. They all laughed.

"It will lay by evening," the fisherman predicted, looking at the sky and the trees to confirm his forecast. "Tomorrow will be a good day. We can fish 'til noon, pack up and tackle that road—get out while it's daylight." He sat, looking down to where he could see the river running clear and shining through and over the grey granite boulders, mossy green near the banks, white with foam by the larger rocks. Unstoppable, determined; tumbling over itself in its eagerness to find the sea, from which it had come. It was like life, he thought. One might delay the head long rush for a moment, a brief respite in an eddy to one side of the main flow, but no more than that. He was content.

THE FACES OF DEATH

Beautiful, peaceful, gorgeous. That's the kind of day it was. Life was absolutely splendid. We finished our breakfast and walked through the resort's colorful gardens to get the fishing gear and cameras from our chalet. Everything seemed perfect. Death wears many faces. Some are so pleasant and nonthreatening that one can be looking the grim reaper right in the eye and be blissfully unaware of it.

With no sense of foreboding, we collected our gear and walked a few feet to the beach, where the gleaming white sand stretched out in both directions, and across it to the shoreline. There was no wind, no cloud in the sky. Miniature foot–high waves washed gently against the sand, and the boat bobbed up and down slightly, pulling casually against the restraining rope in the guide's hand. It was difficult to believe that the calm, blue water, sparkling in the early morning's sunlight so peacefully, was actually the Atlantic Ocean.

The guide—the boat operator with whom I'd arranged to rent the boat for a day had referred to him as "Captain"—greeted us in Spanish and helped us step onto the foredecking and into the boat. It was a fifteen–foot fiberglass outboard, with a forty–horse Johnson motor. I spotted a smaller trolling motor stowed away forward, as we parked our gear, put on dark glasses, and took our seats. The guide—I could hardly think of this twenty–year–old youth as a "captain"—introduced himself as Arturo, and pointing to the youngster who had been sitting quietly beside the motor, explained, "This is my friend Jose. He is ten years old, and wished to come watch you fish. Do you mind if he accompanies us?"

"Not at all. He is welcome," I replied. A huge grin spread over Jose's appealing face. He was small for his age, I noticed, a very cute youngster with curly black hair and brown eyes, his skin a golden tan. Arturo was a handsome Latin type, though the absence of two front teeth gave him a disconcerting appearance when he smiled. He was slim, and not very tall; perhaps five feet seven.

Arturo started the motor, and headed the boat out to sea. It was lovely, really lovely. The ocean was calm, the air clean and warm. We settled back to enjoy the ride. It was twenty miles across the bay to the river, then a short half mile up the river to the lake where we hoped to find some hungry tarpon. We had never been there, had only seen it on a map, but a fishing trip seemed like a nice way to spice up the pleasant time we'd been having. The resort in which we were staying, on the eastern coast of Columbia, had proved an ideal spot for a relaxing vacation—beautiful scenery, comfortable quarters, excellent food, and a wonderful beach—with everything one could ask for, except excitement.

By the time Elizabeth and I had covered our exposed skin with protective lotions the resort had vanished in the distance behind us, and we were cutting steadily through the two–foot swells of open sea. Far off on our left horizon we could barely make out the shoreline of the bay as it curved around toward the point where we would once again encounter it.

In every direction the view was striking in its beauty. No matter which way we looked, there was only blue sky, blue water, shimmering sunlight. We seemed to be the only thing moving on the ocean that morning.

A flight of glittering silver darts suddenly appeared from the swells ahead of us, flew through the air and landed in a cascade of reflected sunlight in the water some twelve feet from where it had appeared. Another group leaped into the air, and another. They looked like small flocks of tiny silver birds, but obviously were fish.

"Pesquitos," Arturo smiled at the wonder on my face. "Los grandes quieren comerlos."

The tiny gleaming silver fish flew through the air in closely bunched schools of eighty to one hundred, like showers of silver jewels as they leaped to escape the attacks of larger fish feeding on them underneath the surface. I decided to try for one of the predators. In moments I had rigged up a rod and reel, put an eight–inch lure on the line, and signalled Arturo to cut the boat's speed down for trolling.

We awaited developments with interest. Anything could take the lure out there, or nothing. For some minutes it was nothing. The little silver food fish had stopped jumping, it was a very large ocean to be blind trolling in. A jerk on the line caught me off guard, the fish hooking himself, actually. It was a rather nonde-script bass–like fish of perhaps two pounds, which I would have gladly released but the lure had three gangs of large treble hooks on it, and several of them had become embedded during the fish's struggles. I took the lure off the line and quit trolling, anxious to hurry on toward the lake where we hoped for more exciting sport. The lure was left loose on the bottom of the boat; that was my third mistake.

The swells were larger now. Ahead, on the horizon, we could see the hazy blur that meant land was not too far off, perhaps ten or fifteen minutes more. Spray was beginning to kick up from the bow as it sliced through the swells. Elizabeth and I moved further forward to avoid it, and Jose climbed up on the side rail near the stern to get a better view. It occurred to me that this was a risky thing for him to be doing, and I considered mentioning it to Arturo. The fact that I only *thought* about mentioning it was my fourth mistake.

It was such a lovely day, the sea so peaceful. I looked about the boat for the first time. It was an ordinary sort of outboard, with the usual low windshield, a split front seat for the driver and side–facing seats behind for passengers. It had a steel pipe framework extending four feet high on both sides which provided support for a canvas roof—when there was one—and to which the boy was clinging. Suddenly I noticed something, or to be more exact, a lack of something. There was no flotation gear anywhere. Not even a seat cushion. That had been my second mistake. It was too late to do anything about it now. The shoreline was only two miles away. I knew Elizabeth would be apprehensive if this was brought to her attention. She did not enjoy exposure to danger, so I decided to keep quiet; alarming her would serve no purpose.

Arturo turned the boat parallel to the shore, and we cruised past the river mouth. We could see the swells rolling in towards the beach, and a series of breakers. They seemed to form in long lines, roll over in crashing splashes and proceed toward the beach as swells again. Over and over, row after row, ten or twelve separate lines of them. "What the hell?" I wondered. Then I realized that there must be ledges of rock lying one after the other underneath the sea, over which the waves were breaking as they made their way to the beach. There was no sign of human life, on land or sea.

We crossed the river mouth about a mile and a half offshore, and I noticed the boat was suddenly moving sideways as well as forward. We were being carried out to sea by a terrific current from the river. It was amazingly strong. On the map, the river had been hardly more than a tiny scriggle. This current was moving seaward at a speed of over seven miles an hour, from the looks of it, and it was more than a mile wide. I never found out how much more, because we turned in toward shore after crossing a mile of it, while we were still in it.

Arturo idled the motor to half speed as we waited just beyond the first line of breakers, until a big swell—at least seven feet high—passed us. As its crest passed under us he accelerated to full throttle, intending to ride in on the back side of the wave. But the motor didn't have enough power to move the boat fast enough against such a current. Helplessly we watched as the wave slowly left us behind. Into the trough we went, then backed up the slope of the following wave as it overtook us. Elizabeth began to look apprehensive. Her small hands gripped the sides of the boat, and her face was grim.

The bow of the boat suddenly pointed skyward, the wave broke and the boat slammed down half sideways like a ton of bricks. Miraculously we did not turn over, but the boat shipped a great deal of water. It was nearly one–third full. Jose, sitting on the rail, was thrown forty feet from the boat, and was rapidly getting further away as the current took him. Despite the danger, there was only one thing to do, and that was turn back for him. He couldn't swim to us against that current. The boat's speed had been halved by the weight of its sudden load of sea water, but we made it around and almost to Jose when the second wave hit us.

This one was even more violent. It tossed all the gear around wildly, threw the gas can—which was attached to the motor by the usual rubber hose—out into the current, and filled the boat over half–full of water. We watched helplessly again while the gas can floated as far away as the hose would permit, stopped as the hose pulled taut, then floated off when the hose snapped. The motor quit, its fuel source effectively disconnected.

I felt something entangle in my pant leg, looked down and saw it was the big lure. One of the three gangs of hooks was fast to my pants below the knee. I was struggling to rip it out as the next wave hit the boat, which by now was dead in the water. My struggles with the hook were futile.

The boat flipped upside down, throwing us into the water, and as the boat tipped over I heard Elizabeth say calmly, "We are going to drown." Nothing more, only that calm statement, made with no sound of fear or hysteria. I saw the boat coming down on our heads, yelled "Stay with the boat!," and went under. "Dear God, keep those iron pipes away from our heads," I prayed. The water felt warm and I started kicking my way back up to the surface. As soon as my head cleared the water, I whirled about looking for Elizabeth. She broke the surface about five feet from me, untouched by the boat or its pipe framework, thank God. "To the boat," I spluttered, and we swam to where it floated, upside down and awash, the bottom barely above the surface, except during the periodic passage of each swell when it was momentarily completely submerged.

It may seem strange that we would swim to an overturned boat that was headed for Iceland, instead of toward a safe beach about two miles away. But Johnny Weismuller couldn't have made it to that beach against the current, not on his best day. Anyway, we caught up with the boat, and I pushed Liz up so that she was lying over the keel crossways. Each wave that came rolling by pushed her back into the water and I had to keep shoving her back onto the boat. The fiberglass bottom was slicker than bear grease, and the "keel" was only a tiny half–inch strip too small to give her a handhold. Liz had kicked off her shoes, having read somewhere that one is less apt to drown without shoes, but I'd been too damn busy to think of mine. There was still at least a pound of junk in my pockets, and about an hour later I was astonished to find that my straw hat was still on my head.

I found that I could keep myself up by treading water, and while pushing Liz back up on the boat bottom, even rest for a few seconds between pushes with a hand on the motor mounts. Arturo was clinging to the bow by now, and Jose came splashing back toward me.

Suddenly the youngster gave a scream of intense pain. What the hell? The tugs I felt on my leg told me what was wrong. In our mutual thrashing around the big lure stuck in my pant leg had somehow gotten the other two gangs of hooks embedded into Jose's forearm. Christ! If I moved my leg at all, Jose screamed in agony. I was twisted like a pretzel, trying to tread water with one leg, and wrenching at the lure to get it out of the pants. I was desperate now, and the adrenaline of terror pulsed in my veins, but I wasn't strong enough to tear the khaki. The lure wouldn't budge.

"Señor, Señor." Jose was sobbing with pain, and pleading with me to not move my leg.

Good God! I could see the red streaks of blood flowing downstream in the current.

"When will the sharks come?" I wondered. "Arturo! Come help us," I yelled.

Arturo swam to us. Even the two of us couldn't tear those blasted pants loose from the lure. Penney's would have been proud of those pants. Arturo dove under and I could feel him tearing at the pant leg with his teeth. Somehow he managed, in spite of his missing front teeth, and I felt the pants come free.

"Oh, Señor," Jose's voice was half–moan, half–sigh as the deadly barbs stopped digging into his arm.

"Well," I thought, "that one's fixed for now. What next?" I was back to treading water with two legs, and keeping Liz asprawl the boat bottom as much as possible. "We must be two and a half miles offshore by now," I thought, "and still going out to sea. Warm water, no discomfort, at least we won't freeze. Warm water, plus blood scent—Jose was still bleeding, and no way to stop it—equals shark. It is only a question of when. We are all tiring, too. Won't be able to keep this up too much longer. Good God, only a few minutes ago— thirty? Or forty? The day was lovely, and we were blissfully happy."

The fiction writers portray their heroes as unperturbed, brave men of clear mind and quick decision, who always came up with the correct solution when faced with deadly danger. Somehow it didn't work that way for me. I was scared to death. My mind had considered all the possible solutions to our predicament— which didn't take long—and there *weren't* any. We couldn't swim out of it; we were getting further and further from land; we couldn't hold onto the boat forever, even if it didn't sink, because it was too exhausting; soon we would be surrounded by sharks. We were going to die.

Liz, who had said not a word since the boat turned over suddenly asked, "Will they save us?" There was a definite note of hope in her voice. For a moment the question made no sense to me.

"*Who*?" I had no idea what she was talking about.

"Those guys in the boats," she said, pointing back over my shoulder toward the beach. I turned and looked.

It was the most beautiful sight I've ever seen, or hoped to see. Four big dugouts were headed toward us. Each had three men in it, paddling furiously. The paddle blades flashed and sparkled in the sun, the water drops brilliant as they flew from the blades. The dugouts plunged and slashed through the wavetops like shining knife blades.

"By God, they'd better," I muttered.

It was a matter of moments until the dugouts were alongside us. One of the men was shouting orders in a strange tongue, and talking to Arturo in Spanish. Then more orders. His dugout picked up Liz and Jose. Another boat came up to me and I was dragged into the middle of it, full to the bursting point with gratitude to these wild–looking people. A third dugout had fished Arturo out of the ocean. More orders from the chief— there was no mistaking his position—and the men in our three dugouts started after the overturned motor-boat. The chief's dugout headed around toward the beach with Liz and Jose. I waved what I hoped was an encouraging wave at her as they left us. She looked quite small and vulnerable. I learned much later that she not only didn't see the wave, she hadn't seen me at all and wasn't sure where I was.

I watched the chief's dugout until it disappeared in the breakers. Meanwhile, the men in our three dugouts were running a salvage operation. Two men in each boat paddled, one swam. Everything that wasn't on the bottom of the Atlantic was picked up and thrown in a dugout. To keep my mind from worry about what was happening to Liz, I decided to study the men and their equipment.

The dugouts were large, over twenty feet long and nearly two feet wide. Chopped out of large trees, they were a good sixteen inches deep. The paddles were larger than any I had seen before. I picked up the one that wasn't in use—its owner was busy swimming after lures, fishing poles, cans, and other floating objects— and was astonished by how light it was. Balsa, I thought.

The men were Indians—Arturo had called them Mosquitos—and I marveled at their skill with the boats. Muscles rippled under the copper skins like coiled springs. No wonder they could drive those dugouts at such speeds. They seemed equally at ease paddling from standing or kneeling positions, though I found the boats to be damned unsteady platforms whenever I tried to change my position.

When everything loose had been picked up from the water, they turned their attention to the motorboat. It took six of them, plus Arturo and me to turn it over, the pipe frames were so heavy. After about ten tries we finally made it. The motorboat sat there upright in the waves, not sinking, but all of it was about six inches under water. Four of them got in the outboard with some of the two pound coffee cans they used to bail out the dugouts and started to bail. Impatient to get back together with Liz, I watched with considerable frustration.

Now, I hadn't demonstrated an intelligence on the genius level so far that day, but I wasn't stupid enough to think anyone could bail the water out of a boat that was *underwater*! Not even the local cavalry, good as they were. "This just can't be done, fellahs," I thought to myself. Which kept me batting one thousand, I was wrong again. Those guys were moving so fast that it looked like a huge pump throwing out water. I still can't figure out *how* they did it, I only know that I sat there alongside and watched that boat slowly move up until the siderails began to show, and then the stern came up, and in about twenty minutes it was riding normally on top of the water.

They lashed it securely between two of the dugouts, and we headed for the shoreline. We must have been at least four miles out by this time. Maybe five. It was a beautiful sight, watching to see nine handsome men drive the dugouts through the swells, paddle blades flashing in the sun. I regretted that my camera was on the bottom of the ocean. The Mosquitos showed no sign of fatigue, though they had been going all out for more than two hours. I wondered how they would manage the breakers which had been our undoing. The cumbersome motorboat would not make the problem any easier, I knew.

They managed it so perfectly that it looked easy. My respect for their seamanship took a quantum leap upward, though it had already been extremely high. They didn't go through the breakers head–on, but rather slid through each line on a slant, waiting to find a short section of the line that was not yet breaking over, and accelerating rapidly to shoot through those calmer spots. It worked with hardly a splash, in spite of the outboard.

As we approached the beach, I could see that we were landing to one side of the river mouth, out of the strong current. There was considerable chatter and laughter from our saviors, who pointed toward a group of people walking across the sand toward the river. Seeing us coming in, the group turned toward us, and to my great delight, I saw Liz walking in the lead. She broke into a clumsy run through the sand and I jumped out of the dugout and ran to meet her.

We were both laughing and crying and talking all at

the same time. To be safe, on dry land, and together again. It was wonderful, fantastic. But it wasn't over yet, our predicament had not been completely resolved.

The Indians motioned for us to head up the beach, away from the river. I hesitated, and Arturo spoke up in Spanish.

"Do as they say, señor. And do not let them know you have any money with you, please."

"Do they speak Spanish, Arturo?"

"Only the chief," he replied. "The others speak only the Mosquito tongue, which I do not understand."

"Where are they taking us?"

"To their village. About a mile up the beach, I think." Arturo was obviously scared.

I remember a brochure I had been reading at the hotel a few nights before, which had mentioned the Mosquitos. Wild Indian fishermen, it had called them, and went on to say that they had been cannibals until twenty–five years ago. Suddenly the wide grins didn't look so reassuring, the filed teeth seemed more menacing. "Thank God I didn't show that brochure to Liz," I thought.

Meanwhile, Elizabeth was having trouble with the hot sand on her bare feet, since her shoes were somewhere on the bottom of the ocean. I took off mine and gave her my wool socks to wear. We must have presented a weird picture tramping up the beach. Jose— and some Indian children—had made up the group who had been with her when we met.

Meanwhile, the dugouts and the outboard were being paddled along the shoreline toward the village, I noticed. By the time we arrived, Elizabeth had filled me in on what had happened to her and Jose during the past two hours. Listening to her accounting, I decided that perhaps I'd had the best of it.

"I didn't see them pick you up," she said, "and wasn't sure where you were, even if you were still alive. They brought us to their village, and of course I couldn't speak their language or Spanish either. The chief cut the big hooks out of Jose's arm and bandaged it, then gave him a shot of penicillin…"

"*What*! Penicillin?"

"Yes, he showed me the label, and seemed quite proud of himself. He kept saying something about the Peace Corps. Anyway, the women all crowded around me so close I could hardly breathe, and touched my hair and my clothes. Several of them touched my wrist watch, and laughed and talked about it. It was pretty awful, and as the time went on I became more and more sure that you must be dead. One of the women offered me a comb, and I tried to comb some of the salt out of my hair. It was something to do to retain my sanity."

"Finally, I decided you would never come, and I'd better start trying to find my way back to the resort. I didn't know what else to do, so I started walking toward the river. The map had showed a highway crossing it, I remembered. Maybe I could hitchhike or something. Anyway I felt that I had to do something no matter how foolish or futile. I motioned Jose to come and we started off. The sand burned my feet, but I was beyond caring about it. Then when we got near the river I saw the boats coming through the breakers and started running toward them. You'll never know the joy and relief I felt at the sight of you—safe and sound and still wearing that ridiculous hat."

We walked up the beach holding hands like teenagers, and I silently thanked whatever Gods were watching over us that we hadn't been five minutes later in arriving—too late to find her!

As we approached the village, the entire population turned out to greet us. The chief came out, took us to his own hut, and offered us some rice, which his wives were cooking on an open fire inside the hut. They were not using any utensils, just laying cakes of mashed rice on the coals. The hut had a dirt floor, and was quite primitive. Looking around, I couldn't help thinking of that penicillin shot.

We refused the food—it didn't look too appetizing—accepted his offer of beer. He informed me that we were even more lucky than I'd thought. They usually fish in the lake, where they are unable to see the ocean at all. Once a month they fish in the ocean. Today was that once.

I asked him to accept my three rods and reels and

what lures were left as a gift. This was actually an idle gesture; they were his by right of salvage anyway. Arturo "gave" him the trolling motor which by some miracle had stayed in the boat through it all. The chief was gracious enough not to laugh at our "offers" and accepted the "gifts" solemnly. He explained to me that I must pay him for the penicillin and also for their time— three hours for twelve men—spent in saving our lives. I assured him that I would be more than happy to do so, but that my money was at the resort. Was there some way we could get to the resort, preferably without leaving dry land?

"Perhaps. I will try to find a taxi. There is a small pueblo on the highway near here. We can walk there now, if you are ready."

The four of us walked with the chief to the pueblo, which had one dingy, dirty bar. Inside the bar we found a rather disreputable Colombian who said he would drive us to the resort in his taxi for thirty dollars, U.S. The taxi turned out to be a pre–WWII Plymouth, which creaked, rattled and knocked so loudly that I was sure it wouldn't make the one block to the outskirts of town, let alone the twenty–five miles to the resort. That kept my record for the day intact, I was wrong again.

Enroute, as we clanked along at thirty miles an hour, I asked Arturo how many times he'd made that run into the lake through the breakers. The marina operator had assured me that our "captain" would be a completely experienced guide, "who knows the lake like the back of his hand, señor." Arturo replied that it was his first trip and, he added emphatically, it would be his last. That was my *first* mistake, believing the damned marina operator.

We arrived at the resort, got the money, paid off the driver and turned to the chief. "How much do I owe you, jefe?"

"Twelve hundred pesos, señor. And twenty extra for the penicillin."

"Will you take more as a gift? After all, you saved our lives."

"No, señor. That is all I will take." The literal translation of his next comment was, "It was not worth more."

In our money, it came to forty–eight dollars and fifty cents, roughly. About twenty–five dollars apiece, if you don't count Jose and Arturo. Which is twenty–four dollars and ninety–eight cents a piece more than our lives had been worth a few hours earlier.

HOW IT ENDS

The sign on the door read "closed." The man got out of his pickup and approached the locked door as he picked out the key from an over–full key case. He inserted the key in the lock, opened the door, and stuffed the bundle of keys in his pocket. The case wouldn't close. "It might close with that key gone," he thought.

The office seemed stuffy. He left the door open, walked over to his desk. It was a mess. The mess looked normal to him; cluttered piles of the past three days' mail, papers, checks, bills, and advertising covered most of it. He sat down, put on his glasses, and began methodically to work his way through it as he had for over thirty years. The wastebasket between his feet began to fill up with discarded junk mail and empty envelopes. As the clumps of mail disappeared, other piles underneath became visible, piles of work that for one reason or another had gone undone, were still pending. Some items of personal mail needed to be set aside to go home for his wife, and he hesitated, not sure where to put them. He decided to put them in the pickup, out of the way.

The mail attended to, he turned to the now uncovered pile of current items, which was not unlike the other piles except for its location in the center of the desk. This sorting took more time than the mail, for he considered each item and its comparative urgency. The large pile dwindled as three new ones grew: urgent items to be done tomorrow; moderately urgent items for the balance of the week; the "as soon as I get time" collection.

He started in on the notes: messages left for him by the secretary or one of the drivers, phone calls to be made mostly. "Harry wants you to call, ASAP." Something to do with the ranch, perhaps: urgent. "Mike Fisher called. Phone him collect at 415–420–4001." That would be about some bonds Fisher wanted to sell: when I get time pile. A note he'd made himself, "Check with Klein on 9–15." A reminder to collect a payment due: moderately urgent pile.

Next he tackled the old unpaid bills: Durham Pump, PG&E, Purity Oil, Collier Hardware, two drug stores, a doctor, an optometrist. The ones which threatened finance charges: urgent. The others: when I get time…and money, the thought came unbidden, and he smiled.

A letter from Africa lay exposed now. A twinge of guilty pleasure went through his guts; it had been there too long. He picked it up and reread it, slowly swiveling in his chair to turn his back on the desk and the work. The letter read, he lifted his eyes to stare, took off his glasses, stuck one of the temple ends in his mouth and chewed softly, gently, feeling with his tongue the indentation in the plastic from countless other chewings. He did not see the broken, dusty venetian blinds that hid the big windows in front of him or the twenty–five–year–old philodendron plant which grew crazily in odd angles in front of them. His gaze was focused far beyond. He was looking at flat–topped acacias scattered on a dry savannah, jumbles of granite–block kopjes, herds of wildebeest and zebra running through the dust; he was hearing the angry trumpet of elephants charging with ears spread wide, the rumbling thunder of stampeding buffalo, the compelling roar of lion at night, the lyric symphony of birds at dawn. Would these wonders be more than memories in his future? His question went unanswered.

The quiet rustle of the letter's falling on the floor reached into his consciousness, and he bent to retrieve it, placed it once again in the urgent pile. A small furrow in his forehead, long established and now irre-movable, deepened slightly as he turned again to the desk.

The clutter was getting worse again, and he decided

to empty one of the desk drawers. Much of its contents went into the wastebasket. He looked at each item as he filled the basket: business cards, hundreds of them in their neat packets; deposit and checkbooks on accounts long closed; invoice blanks for the fertilizer company sold fifteen years before. Then he picked up the overflowing wastebasket and headed for the outside to dump the contents into the 55–gallon garbage drum. The drum was nearly empty, he noted with some satisfaction. Even so, he wondered if it would all fit in. A lot can accumulate in thirty years. He took the basket back to the desk.

The pile of urgent safely stored in one of the drawers, he started in on the pending files. It went faster; only one item, a misplaced bill from the phone company, was transferred to urgent. The remainder would go in a drawer, he decided, but first he must empty another one. Again a casual inventory of no longer useful tools of his trade fell into the wastebasket: envelopes with return addresses of a now nonexistent finance company; an ink bottle so long unused that the ink had dried up—how long since he had used a fountain pen? An address and phone number index that he'd forgotten he owned; a book of blank notes from the finance company days; bills from the oil company on the two wells in which he'd mistakenly purchased a limited interest four years before.

Once a drawer was emptied of its now useless

items, the remaining assortment was consolidated into other drawers. One drawer had dozens of old insurance policy jackets in it. He marveled at the number, tried to think back to the reason for such an accumulation. The logic of his frugality in the matter escaped him, but he was pleased at the additional space in the desk when they had all gone into the wastebasket. Gradually the desktop blotter began to appear, faded green and torn in spots. Once again he had to empty the basket's debris in the big drum outside.

Some things he wanted to keep, of course: a tiny calculator which he never used, the gift of a client–friend; an Oriental letter opener in the shape of a minia-ture samurai sword and scabbard; his stapler and the desk calendar which he used as a tickler file when he could remember to turn the pages. He carefully re-moved paperclips and rubber bands as he discarded, noting with surprise how rapidly they filled the tray in the center drawer of the desk. Some of the things he took to the pickup separately: the in–and–out basket, for as long as he could remember, had only held bills to be paid; the wooden, desktop file holder and its cargo of frequently used files. The adding machine he left on the desk; it needed a good cleaning.

Other things became visible as the desktop emptied: cobwebs, ancient cobwebs covered with years of dust that could not possibly have remembered the days of the spider which made them; dirt and dust thick enough to write in—he traced the word "retire" and then "old," hardly aware of what his fingers were doing, then hastily rubbed them out; small bits of paper on which he had made notes to himself. He read two or three. "Karl C. needs more." The words meant nothing to him now, and he wondered if the tasks for which the notes served as reminders had ever been done. If not, it had made no noticeable difference to anyone. If so, had it mattered? He shook off the thought, turned back to his desk clearing.

The only things left on it now were checkbooks for the current accounts and the life insurance manuals. He stowed the checkbooks in available drawers, exposing some color prints of flood damage to one of his ranches. They had been taken to support a possible suit for damages, he recalled. The ranch had since been sold. He started putting the prints into the discard. One of the sets looked odd, and he stopped to look at the photos more closely: pictures of elephants and lions stretched out on the ground, darted and tranquilized. He sat thinking of his work with the Parks Department in Rhodesia, then dropped the pictures in the basket and headed out to the drum with another load. It was getting full, he saw. He went back to the desk and the manuals. There were old ones, going back as far as 1948. His new quarters at home were too small to permit nostalgia. Only the three current ones went to the pickup; the old ones went out to the drum.

Finished, he sat in his chair, looked at the desk, shook his head. The desk was filthy. He looked at the rest of his cubicle—a corner of space in the office of a butane company he had once owned—rented for twenty–three years from an ex–partner. His space was filthy. He'd known that, of course. The butane office was also filthy and had been since its establishment. Butane customers are mostly poor, and the owner, afraid they wouldn't pay their bills, didn't want them to think he was making money. But the man was looking at the space now as though for the first time, seeing it for what it was. He was surprised. Somehow he hadn't realized how really filthy it was.

He looked at the walls, seeing for the first time in years a map of the city, the street names no longer readable; the quality awards; the merit awards; the Million Dollar Club stickers. He had looked at that wall every day—his calendar hung on it; sitting at the desk, he faced it—without seeing any of these trappings. There was nothing there that he would take, he decided. They were only pieces of paper.

He looked back at the desktop. There was still something on it which had been hidden behind the manuals—a desk pen set covered with dust. Reaching for it, he saw the small brass–framed picture in its swivel case alongside the pen. A child, a photo—black and white—a child peering through the bars of a crib. Who in the world—? Dark, curly hair, it wasn't one of his own, all blonds. Or himself. Maybe his wife, he thought, and wondered about taking it home. All things considered, he decided not and slowly dropped it into the basket. It went "clank" as it collided with metal. He smiled briefly.

He wondered if it were time now to call his son who was to help with the loading and unloading of the pickup. No, there were still two four–drawer filing cabinets and the bookcases to go through. He would wait a bit longer, clean out the filing cabinets first.

The bottom drawer was full of small, policyholder cards, rubber–banded green bundles segregated by area. As he pulled them out of the drawer, several bundles to the handful, he tried to decide if perhaps they had faded too. It was hard to tell; they were all about the same. Slowly, then more rapidly, they made the short trip from drawer to basket. As he took this load to the drum, several packets slid off and fell on the floor; he had to go back for them.

Behind the drawer's partition were stacks of sales brochures. Some of the ones he had made himself, protected by their clear, plastic covers, still looked new. Completely outdated and useless in the modern world of finance, of course, like some other things, but he felt a small glow when he studied them. "They were damned good in their time," he thought, watched them slide smoothly into the wastebasket, and turned to the next drawer.

It was full of copies of typed proposals, sample contracts, wills, agreements, and trust instruments. Dust rose as he leafed through them, and he coughed twice. They represented the musty remnants of battles fought, won, and lost with clients and prospective clients. He read the names as he slowly fed them into the basket: Mead, Kilpatric, Halperin—there were several hundred of them—Foley, Nisson, Thompson. Some were dead now, others retired or bankrupt. Over the years they had been the bigger businesses in town, but time had sought them out one way or another, even the biggest of them. New names ran things in town now.

One of the old names brought a smile to his face: Harry Jenkins. He was more than a client, much more. They had started together, struggled for survival to-gether, in the finance company. Harry had managed the office for him. They had remained good friends as they progressed through the many phases of their business careers. For Harry the phases had been building con-tractor, farmer, orchardist, processor; for him, fertilizer distributor, house builder, butane store owner, cattle raiser, used car manager, farmer, orchardist. Curiously, among all their ventures, only the cattle had been a failure.

Harry's and his relationship involved more than business; however, they were hunters together in the same deer club. He grinned and scratched his head, absentmindedly as he sat staring at the paper but seeing scrubby oak trees, dry grass, manzanita, and lava rocks; a patched and worn tent; a stone grill with a fire glowing down to coals; the moonlight gleaming silver on the meadow as eyes glowed through the dark and coyotes called across the canyons.

He returned to reality grudgingly, throwing all the papers into the basket which was full again. He took it out to empty in the drum. That was full now, too. He had to jam some of the papers down hard to get the lid on.

The new problem—what to do with the rest of the throwaways—occupied his mind for a few moments, and he was grateful. The wastebasket was going home with him; he could fill it one more time and put the contents in garbage cans at home when he arrived. He attacked another drawer and soon had the basket full again. He rose, stretched his back, picked up the basket and adding machine and took them out to put in the cab of the pickup. Back inside, he walked out to the back rooms to look for cardboard boxes. He took three larger ones and returned to his space. For another day, at any rate, it was still his.

The next two drawers were much more crucial than the others had been. These were files, the personal and client files. He must analyze each for its present and future value and throw out only the truly useless. It took time, but in the end he felt satisfied that nothing important had gone into boxes. He had debated over the files regarding the early years of income tax reports dating back thirty–two years. The statute had run out long ago, but it wouldn't hurt to hold them a bit longer; there was plenty of room now in the cabinets. He looked around again, surprised by how different the room appeared now.

Time to call his son. He dialed the number, replied to the "Hello" with a quiet "I'm ready now," was grateful for the answering "Okay, be right there," and its matter–of–fact tone. While waiting, he went back to the side room, found the box of his personal bank statements and took it out to the pickup.

His son looked around the office with undisguised curiosity. The man waited quietly until the perusal was finished.

"The desk ready?" his son inquired. "You're going to take the drawers out of it, aren't you?"

"All but the middle one. The papers in it are too small and loose. We'll put it back in the desk after it's loaded so the wind won't blow them away."

"Okay."

They began by carrying out the drawers of the desk, piling them in the back of the pickup. The desk itself was still heavy, and the man puffed a "whew" when they had it in the pickup. They walked back into the office, stared at the empty space where the desk had been. It was filthy.

The man saw that there were a half dozen rolled up

paper cylinders leaning against the bookcase; they had been hidden before by the desk. He unrolled each of them: three blueprints of solid–set layouts for the orchard he no longer owned; an aerial of the ranch he had sold ten years before; some blueprints of a flood diversion project that had been done on another ranch, sold fifteen years ago. He kept the last, an aerial of the mountain property they owned in a canyon near town. The others were crumpled into one of the boxes, two of which were now full.

"I'll take these to the dump," he said. "Tomorrow maybe."

They tested a filing cabinet. "Not too heavy. We can handle it." They had to go slow with it, finally got it into the bed of the pickup, and pushed it in alongside the desk. "That other one is much heavier. We'd better leave it until tomorrow. Joe can help me with the appliance dolly."

"Good," the son said. "This one was bad enough." The remark brought a brief smile to his father's face.

They walked back inside. The cubicle was beginning to look abandoned to them. The son picked up the chair and took it to the pickup, and the man started in on the bookcase. When the son returned, he was busy throwing volumes into the last box. They were research and reference books: taxes, estate planning, legal volumes, accounting services, bulletins; a few brochures and sales works. Many of them were large, bulky, heavy volumes. His son looked a bit askance at the vicious haste with which he was throwing them away.

"Throwing away my brains," the man said, half to himself. "Never use them anymore now," he added apologetically. The son said nothing.

They carried the bookcase to the car and stowed it.

The man went back for a last look. His son came as far as the doorway and stood there, watching him. The man absorbed it all: the dust, the dirty window, the labyrinth of cobwebs, the vacant area.

"For thirty years," he thought. "It was my sanctuary, my fort, my command post. From this tiny corner of filth and cobwebs, I ran the finance company, the fertilizer company, the various ranches and orchards, and the insurance business." He turned away, started for the door, answered the unspoken question written on his son's face. "I'll see you at home, okay?" He locked the door behind him, got into the pickup, and drove slowly homeward.

He backed into the driveway, noticed the sprinkler was flooding the walkway and shut it off. He looked at the jumble in the pickup, trying to decide where to start. His son had arrived before him—probably inside talking to his mother, the man guessed. He took the full wastebasket, emptied it in the garbage can, and kept going around the house to the big sliding glass door of what had been his den. He opened the door all the way.

As he crossed the threshold, his wife came through the hall door.

"Oh, I don't want a thing like *that* in my home," she said. "I've got plenty of attractive ones you can use."

He looked down at the wastebasket. It wasn't very attractive, but it was big, and it had served him well. Must he part with another friend? "I'll keep it under the desk between my legs. You won't hardly see it," he protested.

She looked at his face, shrugged, and said quietly, "All right."

He hid his surprise and walked into the kitchen. "Let's get it done," he said to his son. They went out to the truck, silently agreeing to take the filing cabinet first. "Don't go too fast for me." His son nodded, concentrating on his own feet.

"Pick a spot fast. This thing's heavy!" his son grunted as they waddled clumsily into the den–cum–office.

"Behind the door." They swung the cabinet back and forth until it settled into the corner, then returned to the truck.

"You want the desk next?"

"Yeah." They wrestled it onto the ground, rested a moment. "I think we'd better take it around through the patio door," the man said. "We'll never get it through that hall door." His wife watched them bring it into the room. "Against that wall." He pointed with his head, breathing heavily from exertion.

"I'll get some furniture polish and clean it up," his wife said. She picked up the desk blotter, handling it like a dead fish. "I'll get a new one of these for you. They don't cost much." He said nothing and walked back with his son for another load. This time it was the bookcase, which they worried into the corner on the other side of the desk.

"It comes up higher than the bottom of the picture." His voice reflected his dismay. He studied the two large pictures on that wall—a leopard on a Tommy kill in a tree, and two rhino feeding with Kilimanjaro in the background. "Can we turn it the other way, in front of the glass?"

"No! I'm not having anything up against that window," his wife replied. "You'll have to raise the picture. Bring in the desk drawers, and I'll fix them." The desk was clean and shiny polished now.

The two men went back to carting in, the remainder of the job not taking much time. When it was finished, he thanked his son, who left, saying, "I've two more sets of papers to correct today. I'd better get home and get started."

The man walked back to the new office, stumbling once or twice over the previous contents of his den which had been placed temporarily in the hall. Motivated by his clumsiness, he decided to find more permanent and less awkward locations for the clutter. His choices were not too successful, but spurred on by admonitions of "I can't have that" and "That will never do" from his wife, he finally moved everything out of the hall. "This intrusion into her home must be trying for her," he thought.

Back in the den–office, he began the task of rearranging his desk and the rest of the room's furniture. His wife's efforts with the furniture polish had made a great difference—everything looked almost as good as new—and they paused to admire her work. He went to the tool closet, took out a hammer and pliers, and returned to work on the pictures. He had no problem with the first, but placing the nail at the right level for the second took three tries before he was satisfied.

His wife went to the patio for the jack phone, unplugged it, brought it in, and plugged it into the jack on the other wall. She paused with the phone in her hand. "It won't go on your desk. The cord would be right across the doorway."

"That's all right. It was never on my desk at the office either. It was on another desk behind me. I'm used to that."

"Oh." Reassured, she placed it on the small desk which he used for film editing. He looked at it, realizing that he wouldn't be able to reach it without getting out of his chair. At his old office he could swivel in the chair and reach it easily, but he said nothing. The readjustment to his intrusion in her life would be difficult enough. He went back to rearranging the desk. The papers began to come out of the drawers and back into piles on the desk top. It looked odd to him, all that wood glistening up at him. The blotter—it came to him—was missing.

The hour was late, almost time for dinner. That time had gone so fast he found incredible. "They don't make days as long as they used to," he thought. He went out to sit with his wife and watch T.V. She was watching *Sixty Minutes*. They did not talk about the moving or the new office. He put it out of his mind. Tomorrow would be soon enough.

In the brittle light of morning, the additions that had taken over his den looked strange, and he felt the changes strongly as he sat in the big easy chair for his daily meditation.

"I think I'll go fishing today. The bills can wait until tomorrow," he told his wife at breakfast.

"I think that would be good," she said. "Bring home lots of fish." He smiled at her and got up to dig his rod, vest, and waders out of the closet. "Do you want me to make you a lunch?" she asked.

"Something light would be nice," he answered. "I mean light enough to be easy to carry in my vest. Maybe a sandwich and an apple."

By the time he had located everything and checked the vest, she had the lunch ready in a plastic bag. He kissed her and started for the pickup. One of the front tires was low. Close inspection convinced him that he could make it to the tire shop all right. The owner, a longtime friend, chatted with him while his tire man repaired and replaced the tire; his conversation was by no means unusual—mostly about how good business had been and worries about collecting delinquent accounts. But the man felt like a spectator, uneasy. He did not mention retiring or moving his office.

When the tire was replaced, he headed for the nearby foothills and the creek. It was midday now, and the sun was hot—well over 100 degrees, he guessed. He parked, put on his wading shoes and vest, took the pole, and started along the trail. It wound around two ridges and then dropped steeply for a half a mile into the creek. By the time he reached the old limestone kiln where the trail dropped off, he was sweating and thirsty. When he reached the creek, it was a relief to sit down on a rock in the shade and rest for a few moments. He decided to wait a bit longer to eat his lunch.

Taking the rolled waders from his vest, he put them on, the shoes over them. The two sections of graphite rod went together; the reel was attached, the line drawn through the guides. He took an old, well–chewed fly— his "super special"—from the fly box and tied it to the leader. He was surprised when the leader end went through the eye of the hook with the first try, for he really couldn't see the eye at all without his glasses. The unexpected success brought a small smile, and he felt that today would be good.

Although he fished it carefully, the first hole produced nothing. "It's too hot," he thought. In the second he caught a small rainbow and in the third a larger one. "Not bad," he thought, "considering it's the wrong time of day and hotter than the hinges." He moved to a shady spot, drank from the creek, and ate his lunch. Afterward he sat, watching the tumbling waters rushing past the grey granite boulders, staring at canyon walls and lava cliffs, conifers and moss–covered oaks growing stark against the blue sky. He was in no hurry. There was nothing more important to do.

Finally he stirred, picked up the rod, and started fishing again. He deliberately passed up good water and cast out only where the mood encouraged him. He seemed to want to make the fishing difficult, to go further than necessary, for some reason. By the time he had his limit, he was a long way up the creek, and started back.

The going was rough: scrambling up and down over boulders, along cliffsides, in and out of water; fighting the brush and grapevines on the sides of the creek. He did not stop until he had arrived at the trail again. He took off his waders, rolled them in the vest, picked up the rod, and started up. The trail was steep and slippery with loose sand and rocks and dry oak leaves. He reached the limestone kiln and went on down the trail without a rest stop, all the way across the ridges to the pickup. Somehow it was important to him to do that.

Feeling tired and relaxed, the man drove home at peace with himself. He took the fish into the kitchen, washed them off, and put them in the refrigerator. His wife looked up from her needlepoint as he kissed her.

"Did you get some fish?"

"Yep. They're in the fridge."

"You'll find your messages and mail on your desk. I'm going to put them there from now on." He felt the muscles tighten in his stomach, said nothing. She did not notice the taut line of his mouth, and when he did not reply, she asked, "Did you hear what I said?"

"Yes. That's okay. A good idea. I was thinking of something." He sat down to read the paper, and by the time she served the dinner, his stomach had relaxed again.

Next morning he meditated again among his office things. He found the trappings strange still and was uncomfortable. After breakfast he went to his desk and began to work: writing checks and paying bills, checking bank statements to balance his savings' accounts. Lunchtime came, and he worked on. His wife watched briefly at the open doorway several times when she passed up or down the hall. He wondered what she was thinking. The adding machine was making noise, a noise new to their home. At one o'clock she came in with a sandwich and some grapes.

"Where shall I put them?" she asked. "Do you want a hard–boiled egg?"

"Oh, thanks." He was surprised and pleased. "Right there on that pile would be fine. An egg sounds good." She came with it, sliced in half and salt and peppered. He worked until three, eating sporadically, until he had finished both the lunch and the work. Picking up the pile of envelopes, he came out into the kitchen.

"One month's bills." He showed her the pile.

"Quite a few," she said. "Where are you going?"

"To the office," he replied. Neither of them realized the incongruity of his answer. "I want to pick up the copier and some other items I forgot to bring home."

He drove to the post office, mailed the bills, and continued to his ex–office. When he walked in, only Joe and Lillian were there. Each of them had worked for the butane company for thirty years. They were old friends.

"Hi," he said.

"Well, you moved out," they greeted him.

"Yeah."

He looked around slowly to the corner that had been his. It had been cleaned, shined spotless. The walls had been washed, the old papers and maps and calendars taken down. The cobwebs were gone. Joe was sitting in the extra desk chair he'd left behind. The rest of the room was as filthy, as cluttered as ever. The man's stomach felt funny.

"Well, Joe, you'll never have to get out of my chair

again when I come in." They all laughed. "I'm leaving that chair for you."

"You forgot your copier," Lillian said.

"Yeah, I know." He thought a moment. "I never use it much actually. Would you like to have it?"

"Yes, if it's not too much money. What do you want for it?"

"Oh, hell, I meant for nothing. I'd like to give it to you."

"Well, sure, but—" she began to protest.

He laughed, went into the safe, got the envelopes with his pink slips, and came out to the main office again. Lillian was pouring the remains of her coffee in the philodendron. "Been watching her do that for twenty–five years," he said to himself. "Damned plant must be hooked on caffeine, probably keeps it alive." For some reason he felt slightly irritated at himself. He noticed that the three large boxes full of things he had thrown away were still sitting where he'd left them.

"There are some perfectly good snap binders and ledgers in there if you can use them," he said, pointing at the boxes. Lillian began to protest about the copier again, and he interrupted her. "Lillian, I'm happy to be able to give you something."

Joe got up and came over to look at the three boxes. "How are we going to know what *you* want out of here?"

The man looked at the reference books and research

materials, the files and records of thirty years. "It's all garbage, Joe. I don't want any of it anymore." A sudden thought struck him. "Could you help me get this file case in my pickup?" They carried it out with no trouble, and returned to the office.

He stood by the counter, his back to the office, and looked out through the big storefront window. It was sunny outside, and he could see the traffic. Outside nothing had changed. As his glance swung toward the door, an object outlined against the window made him blink. "Good God," he thought. He'd completely forgotten. The sign, his sign—all glass, with gold letters, hanging from a golden chain beside the door. "Estate Analyst," it proclaimed to all who passed. He looked at the words below his name, all backwards from inside. It looked better outside.

Well? What in the world could he do with it? He looked back again at the three boxes and shook his head absentmindedly. Maybe someone could use the chain.

"The sign is garbage, too," he told Joe. "See you guys later," He walked out to his pickup and drove home. ────────────